Project Butterfly

Caterpillar Training Guide

Supporting young women and girls of African descent through the transitions of life.

Niambi Jaha-Echols

Perfect Books Publishing

Published by Perfect Books Publishing
7439 S. Bennett Avenue
Chicago, Illinois 60649

Copyright©2010 by Niambi Jaha-Echols. All rights reserved. Printed in the United States of America. No part of this book may be used or reproduced in any manner whatsoever without written permission except in the case of brief quotations embodied in critical articles and reviews without the prior permission of the author.

Perfect Books Publishing, Inc. books may be purchased for educational, business, or sales promotional use. For information please write:
Perfect Books Publishing • 7439 S. Bennett Avenue • Chicago, IL 60649
(773) 457-0114
www.perfectbookspublishing.com

ISBN: 0-9720854-2-4

Cover Design: Niambi Jaha-Echols
Layout: Denise Borel, Borel Graphics, Inc.
Illustrations: Aaron Clarke, Eric Gann, and Niambi Jaha-Echols
Photography: Rod Echols, Living Art Photos

This book is not intended to replace the advice of or treatment by physicians, psychologists, or other health care professionals. It should be considered an additional resource only. Questions and concerns about mental or physical health should always be discussed with a doctor or other health care providers.

**Dedicated to all the
Butterflies in Training**

(hang in there)

What's In Here

Introduction

Phase One: The Egg - My Beginnings

Chapter 1: "Who Do You Think You Are?"
    "What Makes Me, Me?"

Chapter 2: "Rewriting Your History"
    Cultural Definitions of Family
    Who Makes Up The Recipe Called "Me?"
    Your Family Tree

Chapter 3: "What's in a Name?"
    Names - What Does the World Call You?
    The Tapes
    The African Way
    Finding Your African Birth (Earth) Day Name

Chapter 4: "Nobody Understands Me"
    Creating Sacred Spaces (inside and out)
    "Me, Myself and My Third Eye"
    Seeing From the Inside Out

Chapter 5: "What Do I Do When I Don't Know What to Do?"
    Going With the Flow
    "In Order to Maintain Your Creative Flow, Some of the Clutter Has Got to Go!"
    The Energy of Colors
    Mentors & Me
    Tapping Into African Wisdom of the Past
    The 42 Principles of Ma'at

Phase Two: The Caterpillar - Me and My Body

Chapter 6: "What's So Special About Being a Girl?"
        Girl Power
        What's So Special About Being a Girl?
        Protecting Your Sacred Spaces
        Help For Protecting Your Sacred Spaces
        Intuition

Chapter 7: "Why Do I Sometimes Feel Like I'm Going Crazy?"
        Periods, Mood Swings and the Moon
        Cycles of the Moon and Our Bodies
        Depression, Anger and Sadness
        Meditation and the Mothership

Chapter 8: "Taking Care of My Body"
        Food and My Mood
        What Do We Really Need From Food Anyway?
        Is Pork - Black Folks Meat?
        Hygiene

Chapter 9: "What's Wrong With My Hair, and Why Won't It Grow?"
        Me and My Hair
        The Hair Test
        My Personal Hair-Story
        Do YOU Have Good Hair?

Chapter 10: Influences of the Media
        "Lights, Camera, Action. Sorry Ms. Jackson..."
        Music, the Media and My Mind
        "I Want to Look Like the Girls in the Magazines"
        Magazines Don't Always Show You the Truth

Phase Three: The Cocoon - Being With Myself

Chapter 11: "Why Is It Always About SEX?"
    What's Love Got to Do With It?
    Releasing Previous Sexual Encounters (Cutting the Cords)
    Looking for "Daddy Love" in All the Wrong Faces & Places
    Family Life Theatre

Chapter 12: Let's Talk About Boys
    Boys. What's Up With Boys?
    Being a Couple

Chapter 13: "Finding My Posse"
    Choosing Friends
    Gossip
    Drugs/Alcohol
    How Do You Party?
    Loving and Accepting Myself
    Peer Pressure

Chapter 14: "Why Do We Have to Die?"
    "I Just Lost Someone I Really Care About"
    Ways to Remember Loved Ones Who Have Made Their Transitions

Chapter 15: "Help! I Need Some Support Over Here!"
    "Who Are Ancestors?"
    "What Are Rituals, and Why Are They Important?"

Phase Four: The Butterfly - Empowering Myself

Chapter 16: "Connecting With My Life Purpose"
    Identifying My Gifts
    The Potter and the Clay
    Creating Time To Celebrate Your Life
    Working with CP Time
    Procrastination and the Gift of the Present

Chapter 17: "The Flow of Money"
    Making Peace With the Benjamins
    Income vs. Wealth

Chapter 18: "Cultural Diversity 101"
    Dealing with Prejudice and Discrimination
    "How Comfortable Are You With the Skin That You're In?"

Chapter 19: "Beyond The Butterfly"
    "What If I'm Pregnant or Have a Child - Is It Too Late For Me?"
    "What Did You Say Your Baby's Name Is?"

Chapter 20: "Where Do I Go From Here?"
    "Did I Get What I Needed - or Am I Bound to Repeat It?"
    I've Got a Plan

Conclusion
    The Bottom Line Is...
    Appendix: Perpetual Calendar
    About the Author

I am because you are. You are therefore I am.

Introduction

You may be asking, "What is this special fascination with butterflies all about?" There are a number of reasons. We need butterflies to remind us that positive change is possible, and that there is a magic to life. Butterflies awaken our spirits and open our hearts. They give us a sense of hope and the possibility of change. Their ability to adapt to virtually any climate, has made them some of the most successful creatures on earth.

At times you may feel like a Caterpillar and wonder, "**Is this all there is to my life and me?**" The truth is, there is more to you than you can even imagine. Like a caterpillar, you can choose to take the exciting, difficult, inspiring, mysterious, beautiful, spiritual, fun, unpredictable (and sometimes lonely) journey to becoming a Butterfly - but it is definitely your choice. (Remember- all caterpillars don't choose to become butterflies - some get stuck and decide to stay caterpillars their entire lives.) However, because life is like a circle, you can choose to become a butterfly during many different stages of your life. It is a process that you will go through on the inside first, and then it will show on the outside.

My sisters, it doesn't matter what your circumstances are, or if you think that you don't have support. You can overcome any odds that are against you. Sometimes you may feel or think that you are less than others, or inferior. The only thing that you may not have, is a fair chance.

What most of the history books don't tell you, is that your forefathers and mothers were awesome. They were incredibly strong. This training guide will help you to see the truth about who you are and gain power and strength. Know that you are not alone, and you have support, regardless of how it may appear to be.

Many times during your life, people will tell you, "Don't take it personal." Well, this is not one of those times. I want you to take this book very personal. This book is for you.

Some of the information that I am going to share with you may be new to you and some of it you may have already heard. The key to receiving the most from this Guide, is to "wear what fits."

This book is divided into four phases that correspond to the four stages of the complex life cycle of the butterfly. Each stage is important and is specially designed to enable the "Butterfly in the Making" to carry out particular functions. If you find that you are not ready for some of the information, skip to a chapter that feels good to you. You can always go back to that when you are ready.

This is a book that you can use for many years to come. Take your time, and as you grow, you'll find that some chapters will mean more to you than others. And that can change on a daily basis! So be patient with yourself, and I hope you'll find something inspiring to help you on your journey to *"Butterflydom."*

Becoming a Butterfly doesn't just happen overnight. There are the Egg, Caterpillar and Cocoon stages that have to happen first. So, wherever you are - Begin there.

And just like caterpillars, we are hearing our inner call ... ready now to release the past's hold and come forward as beautifully transformed human beings.

Feel free to write or email me. Let me know what you think and how you're doing with the workbook.

Niambi Jaha-Echols
c/o Project Butterfly, Inc.
3543 S. Indiana Avenue
Chicago, IL 60653
Website: www.ProjectButterfly.com
Email: niambi@projectbutterfly.com

"I, being of sound mind and body, but also aware of the uncertainties of anything in life, do hereby make public and declare this Training Guide as something that I will not let intimidate me."

(This is not a contest.)

"Grant me the serenity to accept the things about myself I cannot change. The courage to change the things that I can. And the wisdom to know that I am Beautiful."

last but not least:

"I have the right <u>NOT</u> to remain silent, to put myself first, and be empowered, intelligent and confident - all at the same time. To be fulfilled and happy. Anything I desire that is for my highest good may not be held against me."

DO YOU UNDERSTAND THESE RIGHTS?

"When you teach a man, you teach one

When you teach a woman, you teach a tribe."

-African Proverb

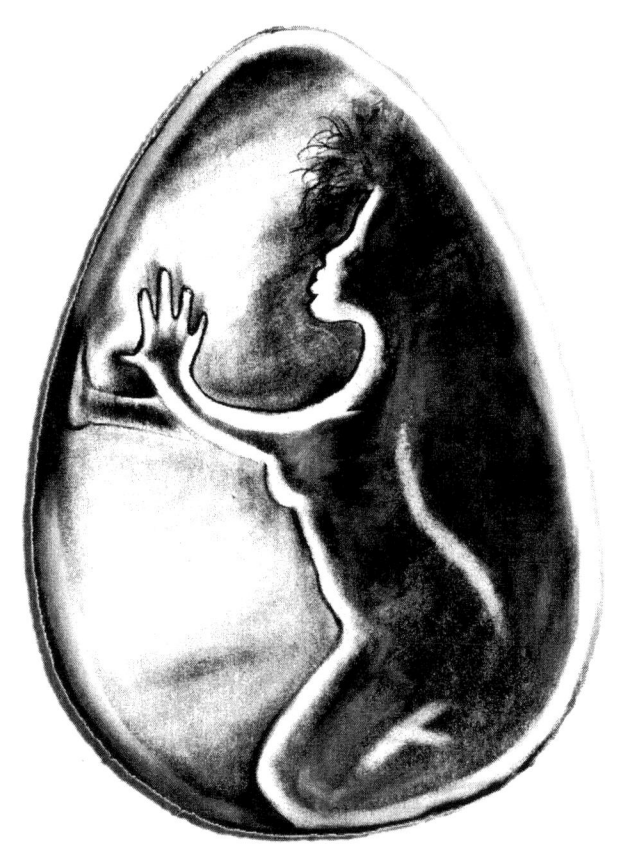

Phase One: The Egg

My Beginnings

— *Chapter 1* —
"Who Do You Think You Are?"

"What Makes Me, Me?"

You are a Spiritual Being filled with an indestructible Life Force Energy. Your Life Force is so powerful that it can be felt by others without them even touching you.

Our ancestors in Africa believed that whenever a family, group, society or the world needs something, somebody is born to provide it. So, rest assured - there are no mistakes.

YOU ARE NOT A MISTAKE!

You were chosen out of the millions of possibilities that could have been. You have a divine purpose and a mission to fulfill that is designed specifically for you. And while you are living on this planet, the Creator has provided to help you with everything you will possibly need for your life's journey - including a vehicle to get around in (your physical body).

Know that there will never be ANYONE who will be able to be a better YOU than YOU!

Say to yourself, and know it to be:
"The Creator had a bright idea - and it was Me!"

The birth canal is the only way to get into this human experience on this planet. When you came here, you came through your mother's womb. Your trip to earth was very much like going away to school. The Creator has given you a full scholarship to the University of Life. Paid in full. When you came here as a spiritual being, you were sent here to accomplish two very important tasks:

- to learn lessons
- to bring gifts

Everybody's curriculum is different. You are a very special project, and you've been given access to the entire planet in order to accomplish your mission. The Creator has also given you a house to stay in while you are here (your physical body), and when it is time, you will return home. Your physical body is a gift. You didn't pay for it - but you do have to take care of it. Your body is not who you are - it is your house. You came here on a special mission with an agenda, plan and purpose. The key is to remember who you are and what your particular mission is.

When we first get here, we are pretty helpless. As babies, we have to depend on others to do everything for us. We have to learn how to speak the language and learn all the rules for being a human being on earth. In all of the excitement of life, sometimes we forget why we even came here, what lessons we are here to learn and what gifts we are supposed to bring. And before we know it, school is over, and it is time to return home.

Don't waste this wonderful opportunity that you have in the University of Life. Pay close attention to you, and REMEMBER TO REMEMBER.

My life deserves my full attention - therefore, I will show up and be fully present for myself.

Life is an unfolding mystery, and you fit in this puzzle called life.

Ask yourself the following question: "I believe I came to earth to...
(Write down your answer in your Project Butterfly Workbook, journal or on a separate piece of paper)

If you can't remember why you came to earth, don't worry. Pay attention to YOU, and it will be revealed sometime during your journey.   Stay tuned ...

— *Chapter 2* —
"Rewriting Your History"

Cultural Definition of Family

There is an old African proverb that you may have already heard that says "It takes a whole village to raise a child." Do you know what that really means? In African culture, children are seen as gifts to the family, group and society; therefore, it is the community's responsibility to help raise the child. Family is not just a husband, wife and children, but includes grandparents, aunts, uncles, cousins, in-laws, and even neighbors and play cousins.

Have you ever noticed that Black people call each other "Brother and Sister" even if they are not related? It's because we are all interconnected. During slavery, black people were forced to leave Africa and be scattered all across the planet (especially in America and the Caribbean). Because we were not able to stay connected with our families in Africa, we formed new families with new sisters and brothers. Our early ancestors had to love, protect and help each other in order to survive slavery. Today we still have to love, protect and help each other in order to survive.

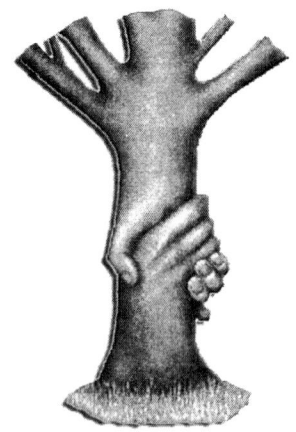

Who Makes Up the Recipe Called "Me?"

My mother

My father

My grandmothers

My grandfathers

My great grandmothers

My great grandfathers

My great, great grandmothers

My great, great grandfathers

My great, great, great grandmothers

My great, great, great grandfathers

My great, great, great, great grandmothers

My great, great, great, great grandfathers

My great, great, great, great, great grandmothers…

Your Family Tree

I'm sure you've probably heard of "Family Trees", and trees are just like people - no two are exactly alike. Your Family Tree may look different from that of other families, or it may look the same. Your family tree may be similar to the inside of a tree.

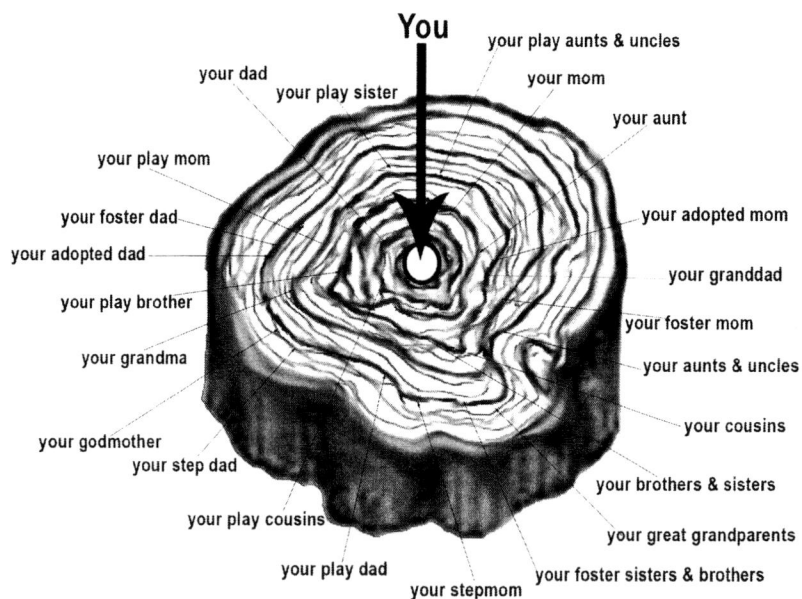

Remember, you showed up on the planet to do a special job. Sometimes our birth families are with us our entire lives and sometimes they aren't. But no matter what - you are never all by yourself. The Creator loves you so much, that He sends you people that may become your family in a different way.

New family circumstances become additions to our lives and not substitutions or subtractions of others.

Trees have rings and each of those rings can represent all of the different family relationships that you have.

Remember - No two Family Trees are alike! And just like trees, families grow and change.

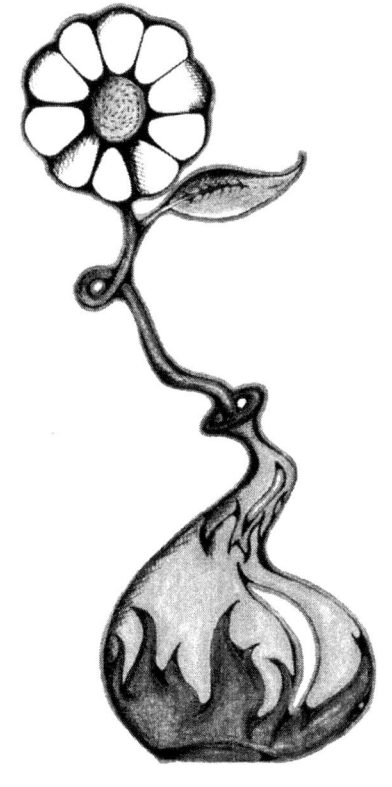

— *Chapter 3* —
"What's in a Name?"

Names

*"When you were born, your parents gave you a name.
The universe gave you a name and a day."*

Why are names so important? Why does it matter? Names are important because they help to identify us, set us apart and can even affect our behavior. For instance, when we call a "chair" a chair, we expect it to be something that we can sit on. We wouldn't call a refrigerator a chair. The word "chair" not only is the name, but it also describes what it is and even what its purpose or function is.

The same thing applies to what we respond to or call ourselves internally. If you allow the world to call you stupid, ignorant, fool or the B____word, that is how, on some level, you will view yourself and how others will view you. That is what self-esteem is all about. How do you view you?

Here is something you can do. I call it **"The Tapes"** and it can be helpful in really uncovering what's on the inside of you. To do this exercise you will need:

- your 'Reject' names list
- a full-length mirro
- a marker
- masking tape

(If you don't have masking tape, use any kind of tape and pieces of paper). **This exercise is best done when you are by yourself.**

The Tapes

On a piece of paper, write down all the titles that you have ever had (for instance: daughter, sister, granddaughter, cousin, friend, aunt, student...).

Then, look at your list and write down ALL of the names that you have ever been given or called during your life. Write them all down - the good, the bad and the ugly. Don't leave ANY of them out. Use your "titles" list to help you remember them all. For example, "my grandmother calls me_____." Just write down the name (not who called you it).

On one side of paper write the word "Accept" and on the other side of the paper write the word "Reject". Now look at your list of names, and on a piece of paper, make two columns. Decide where to put each name - either under the 'Accept' or 'Reject' column. Don't leave ANY of them out.

Now, look at your 'Reject' list and write the first word directly on the masking tape. Tear it off the roll and stick it on your body somewhere. Do that with EVERY word on your 'Reject' list. Don't leave any of them out.

After you have written all of the names from the 'Reject' list directly on pieces of tape (or pieces of paper and any kind of tape) and stuck them to parts of your body...look in the mirror. These are the names that you may be wearing. Look at each one and decide if it's true. Ask yourself, "Do I want to reject this because I don't like it?" or "Do I want to reject this because it's not true?" BE HONEST. You can only remove it if you really don't like it AND it's not true.

For each name that you have taped to your body, look yourself in the eyes and say the following statement, "I reject _____(pick one) because I don't like it and it is not true. I am not a _____." After you say it (and you believe it) then remove that piece of tape from your body.

You may find that some names, even though you don't like them and they are not true, will be harder to remove than others. Say the statement until you believe that you are telling the truth about it and that you REALLY are rejecting it.

Unfortunately, people are going to try to stick names on you for the rest of your life. Sometimes it will be names that they have stuck to them and they don't like - so they try to stick them on you! Other times, it will be names that people will try to put on you if they are angry, jealous, mean or just misinformed.

If someone is angry at you, for example (regardless of who it is), they may try to put some old tape on you that somebody may have stuck on them and they don't like it - so they try to stick it on you. You won't "wear" any of them, only the ones that YOU believe are true about you. So watch what may be trying to stick to you.

DON'T ACCEPT SOMEBODY ELSE'S OLD TAPE!

You may find that you have to do this exercise many times - even in one day. Sometimes you'll be able to tell the person to their face, "Don't be trying to put your negative tape on me!" But many times, you may have to do it when you are alone and able to look at yourself in the mirror. Look in your eyes and see if their tape is stuck to you. If it is, tell yourself that you reject it until you believe it.

You can't stop people from giving you names, but you can decide what you will accept as true.

What do YOU call YOU?
What is REALLY stuck to you?

Check out the "names" and attributes below and see if you can let some of these stick on you.

- Friendly
- Beautiful
- Wise
- The Intelligent One
- Smart
- Strong
- Brave
- Creative
- Confident
- Talented
- Peaceful
- Leader
- Precious
- Joyful
- Queen
- Loveable
- Happy
- Wealthy
- A Gift from God
- Incredible
- Attractive
- Deep
- Spiritual
- Amazing
- Honest
- Truthful
- Trustworthy
- Kind
- Original
- Funny
- Determined
- Enthusiastic
- Energetic
- Sensitive
- Persistent
- Independent
- Insightful
- Perceptive
- Innovative
- Dynamic

The African Way

In many African societies, the day of the week you were born is very important. Our ancestors in Africa believed that whenever a family, group, society or the world needs something, somebody is born to provide it. Your life purpose was (in part) determined by the day of the week you were born.

Usually, a young girl receives a name when she is born and then again when she goes through a rites of passage and becomes a woman. Your name that is based on the day of the week you were born, is yours regardless of whether or not you are able go through a rites of passage ceremony.

Finding Your African Birth (Earth) – Day Name

Use the table in the back of the book to find out which calendar you should use to identify the day of the week you were born.

Then use the Perpetual Calendar (also in the back of the book) to find out which day of the week you were born on. For example, if you were born June 4, 1984, you would use calendar "H". Then find June 4th. In 1984, June 4th was on a Monday.

On a following pages, you can choose one of the African names for the day of the week you were born.

Sunday Child:

Esi (pronounced) eh-SEE

Akosua (pronounced) ah-KOH-soo-ah

You are a born leader

You are dependable and there for those you love

You listen to and love people and they listen to and love you

You see the positive in others and support them in being their best

Monday Child:

Adwoa (pronounced) ah-dwoh-AH

Adjua (pronounced) ah-jew-ah

You know who you are and can see the positive in your mistakes

You hardly ever get bored

You are good at bringing people together for the higher good

People like being around **you** because you bring out the best in them

Tuesday Child:

Abena (pronounced) ah-beh-Nah

Adowa (pronounced) ah-doh-WAH

You inspire others by just being you

You are unstoppable and determined

You work well with others in achieving a common goal

You are not afraid to take risks, even if it leads to change and uncertainty

Wednesday Child:

Kukua (pronounced) koo-KOO-ah

Akua (pronounced) ah-KOO-ah

You are full of love and compassion

You heal and inspire others through your words

You are supportive and your loved ones are always at the top of your list

You are confident and have a strong sense of who you are.

Thursday Child:

Aba (pronounced) ah-BAH

Yaa (pronounced) YAH-ah

You have the capacity to far exceed normal limitations when you are doing what you are destined to do

You are strong and have a lot of will power

You bring out the best in others

You can be a strong leader socially and politically

Friday Child:

Mwajuma (pronounced) 'm-wah-Joo-mah

Efia (pronounced) eh-FEE-ah

Afua (pronounced) ah-FOO-ah

You are a creative visionary

You are not a quitter

You can anticipate things happening before they actually occur

You know that your life has purpose and meaning and you understand and accept that it might not always be easy

Saturday Child:

Ama (pronounced)   ah-mah

Mama (pronounced)   mah-MAH

You are wise beyond your years

You have a deep spiritual quality

You are peaceful and happy because you can see the big picture

You help others to stay calm during the storms of life

— *Chapter 4* —

"*N*obody
*U*nderstands *M*e"

Creating Sacred Spaces
(inside and out)

"Whatever you pay attention to will grow more important in your life" (including you).

It is very important to remember that you are a Spiritual Being. Because the more you remember, the more you will realize that your physical body is just the vehicle that the Creator has given you to use. So, in other words, you have a physical body, but you are not your physical body. The most important parts of you are truly on the inside.

During your life's journey, all kinds of things are going to happen to your physical body (both good and bad). Some things you are going to be able to control, and some you won't. For example, if you were in a car and it hit a tree, the paramedics wouldn't come and take the car to the shop, but they would be concerned about the people inside the car. Your physical body (your vehicle) may get damaged (and that's important because you need your vehicle), but the most important thing is to make sure that you are ok on the inside (your spiritual body.) Remember, you came here for a special purpose and to fulfill a special mission that only YOU can do. Because of that, you have many SACRED Spaces on the inside.

What does "Sacred" mean? It means, "set apart for a special purpose." How will you know what your special purpose is? Through prayer and spending time listening to YOU. There are many surprises and gifts inside of you that the Creator has placed in special places. One of your jobs will be to go on Treasure Hunts on the inside of you and find all the wonderful and special things that the Creator has placed in you. That is why Journaling is so important.

What is Journaling?

Journaling is simply listening to yourself - and knowing that what you think and feel is important enough to write it down. Journaling will teach you one of the greatest lessons that you will learn on your journey - and that is learning to spend time listening to your own inner voice. You came to this planet complete, and there is a wisdom that resides deep inside of you. The more time you spend writing and listening to your inner self, the more you will begin to understand how truly Sacred you really are.

Journaling is listening to yourself and knowing that what you think and feel is important enough to write it down. Any notebook or groups of paper can be used as your journal (you can buy a fancy one in the store, or you can be creative and make your own - either way, it's all good). The most important thing is to begin writing.

Think about all the things we've talked about so far and write out your thoughts in your journal or you can use the *Project Butterfly Workbook*. (Don't worry if you don't have complete sentences or if you misspell something - if you understand what you mean - that's all that matters.)

"Me, Myself and My Third Eye"

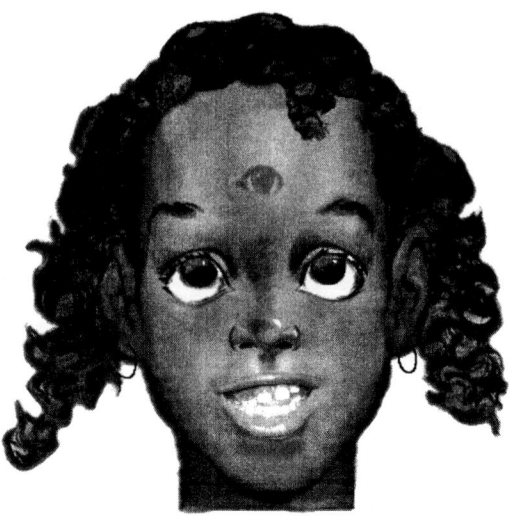

Your Spiritual Body is similar to your physical body in that just like you have physical eyes, you have a spiritual eye. Some people call it your "Third Eye" and some call it your "mind's eye." You use your third eye to see in your mind, your imagination and even into the universe. Your spirit gives you a direct link to the Creator. You can use your third eye to create an idea, a picture or a feeling of anything that you want to happen. You can use it to imagine yourself doing lots of things like: feeling better when you are sick, doing well on a test, feeling confident, or achieving your goals.

Seeing From the Inside Out

You use your mind's eye all the time naturally when you daydream. Creative Visualization is just like daydreaming, only you don't just let your mind wander - you gently guide it to where you want it to go.

Try this very simple exercise: think of something that you would like to improve in your life. Find a quiet place where no one will bother you for at least 15 minutes. Get in a comfortable position either sitting or lying down on the floor. Make sure you are comfortable - but not too comfortable that you fall asleep.

Squeeze, tense and tighten yourself mentally.

Now relax.

Ever notice how babies breathe when they are sleeping? They practically use their entire body. They breathe from their bellies. That is the way you should breathe (especially when you want to 'Relax').

Squeeze, tense and tighten yourself emotionally.

Now relax.

Squeeze, tense and tighten your entire body.

Now relax.

Let all the tension flow completely out of your body. Breathe in deeply, filling up your belly with air and then slowly and gently let it all out. Keep repeating this until you feel every part of your body relax. (Now your mind is probably going to want to think about EVERYTHING - so be patient with yourself.) Focus your mind on you and your body and gently bring your thoughts back each time they wander.

When you feel completely relaxed, begin to think of the thing that you want to improve. Imagine yourself in that situation and everything happening just the way you want it to. Think of all the details, including how you are acting, what you are wearing and how you are feeling. Keep slowly breathing - nice and deep. As you see yourself being and acting the way that you desire, say to yourself "I now make room for this or something better to become real in my life."

Do this exercise only as long as you feel comfortable. And repeat it as often as you can.

Creative Visualization cannot be used to control others or to secretly try to get others to act in a certain way. The Creator gave you your third eye to help you to be your highest self. If you are not sure what the best or highest thing is, ask your spiritual self to show you. Focus your attention on your third eye (right in the middle of your forehead).

— Chapter 5 —

"What Do I Do When I Don't Know What to Do?"

Going With the Flow

One of the hardest lessons that we have to learn, is the art of being by ourselves and with ourselves. Humans spend an enormous amount of time and energy trying to get "people attention." When we think about how big the planet is, sometimes it can be difficult to imagine being here alone. The secret to being with yourself, is knowing that you are never completely alone. It is important to understand our relationship to water, air and Mother Earth. The more we connect to the earth, the more we learn about ourselves.

Water is a wonderful gift that connects us all. Did you know that over two-thirds (that's about 70%) of your body is water? And over two-thirds of the planet is water as well. It is no coincidence. That is why we feel good when we are near water (unless we have had some bad experiences around water that our spirit still remembers). Water and our bodies are the same. It is just like taking a container or glass to the ocean and putting ocean water in it. If you were to look at the glass, what would be in it? Parts of everything that is in the ocean. Everything that makes up the ocean is now in that glass. Everything. Our bodies are like that glass of water - they are our containers. The water was separated from the bigger body of water, but was still part of the ocean, only it was now in a glass (or body),

There are many different types of containers. And just like the glass of water and the ocean, we all have different containers that we are given to use while we are here on this life journey. The only thing that separates me from you is the container that I am in. I'm made up of the same stuff that you are made of. The same stuff. But just like with that glass of water, - what makes us different - what makes our experiences in life different are the containers that we are in. That is the only difference. Some people get to be in champagne glasses, tumblers, or mugs. Some people get to be in a glass that may already have some stuff in it. It is not just a clean glass. It may have all kinds of different particles already in it. So once that mixes with the water, it is no longer just water.

Just like when you make any kind of drink - the base of it is water. To make tea, coffee, kool-aide or soft drinks, water has to be added. But they are all very, very different drinks. They all have different additives. They are all drinks, but if you break them down, you'll find they all started with water. That is why our experiences in life can be all different, even though we are all the same. Made of the same stuff - water. We can have different experiences in life because we are in different containers. The ingredients that we have in our lives help to create these differences.

Water is made up of H2O and there are some basic human ingredients that we all share - that make us human. And it all starts with the basic ingredient -
Water

Water can also remind us that we are connected to something larger than ourselves. A small piece of something bigger.

"In Order to Maintain Your Creative Flow, Some of the Clutter Has Got to Go!"

Have you ever noticed that the more organized you are the better you feel? There is a definite connection between our physical, emotional and spiritual well-being. Sometimes, when you feel blocked, overwhelmed and uncreative, making simple shifts and changes in your environment can mean a lot. When you are unable to think, and you feel trapped and uninspired, check and make sure that your environment isn't contributing to your mood. (Now I know that sometimes we aren't the ones making the mess, but do the best you can with the space that you are truly responsible for.)

There is an old saying, "Cleanliness is next to Godliness," and that is really true. What happens on the outside affects what goes on on the inside. Cleanliness helps to keep all your lines of communication open and clear. Clearing out clutter in your physical space also clears out clutter in your spiritual space.

Have you ever said or felt like, "I need some space so that I can clear my head." When things are loud, confusing, chaotic or cluttered, it's hard to think straight and it creates much stress. It's like trying to hear your favorite song on the radio when the room is full of people talking, and the radio is not completely on the station, so there is lots of static. You have an internal radio inside of you. We are constantly picking up on or tuning in to the messages in the air. Have you ever experienced hearing a song in your head and before you have the opportunity to sing or hum the tune out loud, the person you are with begins singing it? The universe is continuously broadcasting messages to us as well. Just because you can't hear it, doesn't mean that music isn't playing - you're just not tuned in to the right frequency or station.

When you need some Divine inspiration, you have to tune your internal radio to the right station and take time to listen. Cleaning up helps you to think straight and opens you up for new ideas to flow through.

Don't constipate your spiritual flow with physical stuff that needs to go.

Cleaning up helps you to think straight and opens you up for new ideas to flow through.

Make room in your life by getting rid of things that don't serve your higher purpose.

The Energy of Colors

The energy colors carry or what colors to wear when you want support in feeling a certain way.

Green   The color Green is associated with abundance, prosperity, new life and new beginnings. It is a calming color, in fact people waiting to appear on television often wait in a "green room" to help them relax. Wear green when you want to feel balanced, compassionate, generous and alive.

Red   The color Red is associated with courage, love, passion, creativity, excitement, intensity and self-confidence. It is an emotionally intense color and can stimulate your heart beating faster. Wearing red will definitely get you noticed.

Pink   The color Pink is associated with feelings of self-love, self-generosity, attraction, and love. Wear pink when you want to feel loved.

Black   Contrary to popular belief, the color Black is neither good nor bad. It is the absorption of all colors, therefore it does not radiate any vibration of its own. It absorbs energy and has nothing to do with a person's individual character, or goodness (and besides, most black women look good in it).

White   The color White is associated with purity, truth, sincerity, virtue of all kinds, and the highest Spirituality. (Like the color Black, it has nothing to do with a person's individual character, goodness or superiority.

Blue   The color Blue is associated with peace, relaxation, harmony, happiness, joy and clear communication. Because of it's relaxing qualities, people often paint their bedrooms blue. Blue is a good color to wear to a job interview because it can symbolize loyalty.

Brown   The color Brown is associated with a feeling of earthiness. It is a good color to wear or have around you when you need to concentrate or study.

Purple   The color Purple is associated with wisdom, royalty, dignity, and spirituality. Wear it when you want to feel more like a queen.

Yellow   The color Yellow is associated with creativity, clear thoughts, self-confidence and optimism. ("You are my Sunshine…")

Orange   The color Orange is associated with dreams, enthusiam, fun, stimulation and friendship. Wear orange when you are feeling depressed, lonely or bored.

Gold   The color Gold is associated with prosperity, great fortune, spiritual power and understanding. (It has a more masculine energy than silver).

Silver   The color Silver is associated with victory over evil, stability, neutrality and prosperity. (It has a more feminine energy than gold).

Mentors & Me

Success can have many different faces, but one thing is for sure, successful people don't just drift to the top of the mountain. It starts with the decisions you make when you are young. Even some of the things you think may be really insignificant can affect the rest of your life and the choices you make.

One way to **"Bridge the Generation Gap"** is to ask a woman who serves as a role model for you to answer the following questions. Some of the answers you may already know, and some you may be surprised by. Either way, there is only one way to find out...ASK!

When you were a child:

- What was your birth family like?
- How many sisters and brothers did you have?
- Where were you born (at home, in a hospital, etc.)?
- Where did you go to school?
- How was your health?
- What was your favorite thing to do as a child?
- Who was your best friend as a child?
- Did you have any pets?
- What was your favorite game to play?
- What was your favorite food?
- What was your favorite subject in school?
- Did you grow up in an apartment or a house?
- Did you go to church? Did you enjoy it?

When you were a teen:
- Where did you go to high school?
- Did you date?   How old were you?
- Who was your favorite singing group?
- What was your favorite subject in school?
- Who was your best friend?
- Did you have any pets?
- How did you dress as a teen? Do you have any pictures?
- Did you play sports?
- What was your first job?
- Did you get along with your parents?
- What was your favorite food?
- Who was your first love?
- Did you have to make decisions about sex?
- Did you travel?
- What was your favorite TV show?
- Did you have someone to look up to?
- When did you learn how to drive?
- How was your health?
- Did you go to church? Did you enjoy it?

As an Adult:
- Have you ever met anyone famous?
- Did you go to college or work?
- Did you get married? How old were you?
- Did you have children?
- What was the greatest gift you have ever given?
- What was the greatest gift you ever received?

- What was your first major purchase?
- How old were you?
- Did you like your job?
- Where did you live?
- Where did you feel most at home?

Using your creative visualization skills, creativity and imagination, project your mind's eye into the future and go back and answer any of the questions that you have not experienced as a teen or young adult. What do you see in your future?

Tapping Into African Wisdom of the Past

There may be times in your life when you will not know what to do. You may be able to talk to an older person (like your grandmother) or a Mentor. But what if they are not available? Our African Mothers and Fathers used to tell stories and proverbs (using mostly animals) to communicate history, solve problems and to make you think and laugh at the same time. There is a lot of wisdom in African sayings.

See if you can understand the double meaning in each of the following African proverbs and see how these proverbs can be applied to your everyday life:

Ashanti

"Only when you have crossed the river, can you say the crocodile has a lump on his snout"

•

"If you are in hiding, don't light a fire"

•

"One falsehood spoils a thousand truths"

"Do not call the forest that shelters you a jungle"

•

"Hunger is felt by a slave and hunger is felt by a king"

•

"Two small antelopes can beat a big one"

•

"Do not try to cook the goat's young in the goat's milk"

Ethiopia

"One who recovers from sickness, forgets about God"

•

"The frog wanted to be as big as the elephant, and burst"

•

"Unless you call out, who will open the door?"

•

"When the heart overflows, it comes out through the mouth"

•

"Confiding a secret to an unworthy person is like carrying grain in a bag with a hole"

•

"A loose tooth will not rest until it's pulled out"

•

"He who conceals his disease cannot expect to be cured"

•

"Anticipate the good so that you may enjoy it"

•

"When one sets a portion for oneself, usually it is not too small"

•

"When the webs of spiders join, they can trap a lion"

Guinea

"Around a flowering tree, one finds many insects"

•

"The toad likes water, but not when its boiling"

•

"A camel does not joke about the hump of another camel"

•

"A cow that has no tail should not try to chase away flies"

Kenya

"He who does not know one thing knows another"

•

"Try this bracelet: if it fits you wear it; but if it hurts you, throw it away, no matter how shiny"

•

"He who is unable to dance says that the yard is stony"

•

"Absence makes the heart forget"

•

"There is no phrase without a double meaning"

•

"Thunder is not yet rain"

Madagascar

"Indecision is like the step child: if he doesn't wash his hands, he is called dirty; if he does, he is wasting the water"

•

"The end of an ox is beef, and the end of a lie is grief"

•

"Don't kick a sleeping dog"

•

"Don't be so much in love that you can't tell when the rain comes"

•

"If you try to cleanse others - like soap, you will waste away in the process!"

•

"The dog's bark is not might, but fright"

Buganda
"If you burn a house, can you conceal the smoke?"

•

"He who is bitten by a snake fears a lizard"

Niger
"Ashes fly back into the face of him who throws them"

Duala
"The tracks of the elephant cancels those of the antelope"

Moussi
"Little by little the bird builds its nest"

Zimbabwe
"The monkey does not see his own hind parts, he sees his neighbors"

Malawi
"One little arrow does not kill a serpent"

•

"Do not be like the mosquito that bites the owner of the house"

Nigeria

"The cock crows while the idle person grumbles"

•

"The bird flies high, but always returns to earth"

•

"When the mouse laughs at the cat, there is a hole nearby"

•

"Not to know is bad, not to wish to know is worse"

•

"When one is in trouble, one remembers God"

Liberia

"Cock says, 'If there is no one to praise you, praise yourself'"

•

"Mosquito says, 'If you want a person to understand you, speak in his ears'"

•

"Sheep says, 'To report a thing promptly avoids embarrassment'"

Sierra Leone

"A cow must graze where she is tied"

•

"A big fish is caught with big bait"

•

"However full the house, the hen finds a corner to lay in"

•

"Quarrels end, but words once spoken never die"

Senegal

"Cross the river in a crowd and the crocodile won't eat you"

•

"When you know whose friend he is, you know who he is"

•

"If a centipede loses a leg, it does not prevent him from walking"

Rwanda Burundi

"When the leopard is away, his cubs are eaten"

•

"In a court of fowls, the cockroach never wins his case"

•

"Proverbs are the daughters of experience"

The 42 Principles of Ma'at

In ancient Kemet (Egypt), the 42 Principles of Ma'at were a moral code that people used to live peacefully and harmoniously with each other. These universal principles will always remain true throughout time. In fact, all of the Biblical Ten Commandments can be found within them.

Having the right relationship with ourselves, others, nature and the world, creates balance between our inner and outer worlds. By practicing these principles and including them into our daily lives, we have a very real guide to strengthen our character and have the ability to live a more fulfilling, real, empowered and abundant life. (Try it for yourself. What do you have to lose?) Think about how they can be applied to your life on a daily basis, or to current life situations. I've done the first one for you.

42 Principles of Ma'at

1. **I will not do wrong.**

In slang, we have a saying "Girl or (Boy), you know you wrong." When we say that, it is usually with a wink or a smirking kind of approval of another's actions or words. Usually it's because someone has done or said something that we know is not right, but still we kind of give a nod of approval. Rather than correct the person, we agree. When we agree with wrong or inappropriate actions we are just as guilty. Because in a way, we say the behavior is ok. So, to say that "I will not do wrong," but yet I agree with wrong behavior, makes me wrong within my heart and my heart is where my character resides. So it's not just about wrong "actions", but also thoughts, words and deeds.

One of the reasons, I suppose, this is the first of all the principles, is because it includes all of them. In order to "not do wrong," you have to know what is right.

2. I will not be violent.
3. I will not steal.
4. I will not kill.
5. I will not steal food.
6. I will not cheat anyone out of offerings.
7. I will not cause anyone to believe something false.
8. I will not tell lies.
9. I will not waste food.
10. I will not cause anyone or anything pain.
11. I will not close my ears to the truth.
12. I will not commit adultery.
13. I will not cause anyone to shed tears.
14. I will not abuse my sexuality.
15. I will not act spitefully.
16. I will not destroy land that could be used to grow food.
17. I will not steal anyone's land.
18. I will not eavesdrop.
19. I will not falsely accuse anyone.
20. I will not do anything that is offensive to my sacred spaces.

21. I will not seduce anyone's husband or wife.
22. I will not do anything harmful to my body.
23. I will not terrorize anyone.
24. I will not pollute the earth.
25. I will not burn with rage.
26. I will not curse God.
27. I will not cause anyone grief.
28. I will not cause a disruption of peace.
29. I will not act hastily or without thought.
30. I will not overstep my boundaries of concern.
31. I will not exaggerate my words when speaking.
32. I will not do evil.
33. I will not initiate a fight.
34. I will not pollute or waste water.
35. I will not speak angrily or arrogantly.
36. I will not curse anyone in thought, word or deed.
37. I will not place myself on a pedestal.
38. I will not prejudge.
39. I will not steal from or disrespect the deceased.
40. I will not mistreat children.
41. I will not act arrogantly.
42. I will not mistreat animals.

One way to practice the Principles of Ma'at is on a daily basis.

In the morning when you wake up, take a few minutes to relax your body, mind and spirit. Read each of the Principles out loud starting with "I will not.." and then go and have a great day.

Right before you go to bed at night, read the Principles again, this time starting with "I have not..." Check to see how you did each day. Write how you did in your journal.

Aim to be the Best YOU!

The measure of a woman's true character is what she would do if she knew she would never get caught.

Because…

You are what you are –
when nobody is looking

Phase Two: The Caterpillar

Me and My Body

"If there is no struggle, there is no progress."
- Frederick Douglass

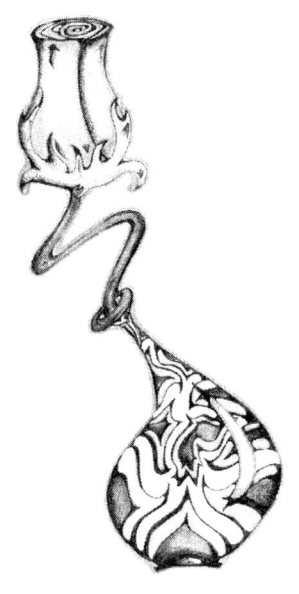

— *Chapter 6* —

"*What's So Special About Being A Girl?*"

Girl Power

Being born a girl child, you have a lot of magic and power around you. You carry the seeds of all the generations in your family to come. You are like an apple.

Go and get an apple. Cut it open and look at all of the seeds that are in that one apple. Count the seeds. Now take a breath. How many apples are there in each of the seeds? You are the apple that carries all of your family line seeds. Each seed can produce hundreds of apples and in each of those apples are more seeds. That is one of the reasons that you are so special and precious to the Creator and the planet.

What's So Special About Being a Girl?
What Are Some of the Benefits?

- You have been given the awesome responsibility to reproduce, guide and nurture the human family

- You have a special creative hookup with the Creator through your intuition, your uterus (which is your creative center) and your spirit

- You should be respected and treated like a Queen

(Just to name a few)

Can you think of any other things that make you special as a girl?

Because you carry the seeds for your family-line within your Sacred Space, how you take care of your body, mind and spirit is very important. The decisions you make affect many, many, many generations to come. So make good and healthy choices not only for yourself, but also for your children, and their children and their children's children. Honoring yourself and your Sacred Space is important because you have gifts to bring and a special purpose to fulfill.

Your body is your mobile home to get around in while you are here on earth, and just like any other vehicle, you have to maintain it (because it's the only one you get). You have to protect it (the best you can) from things that are harmful. And you have to love it because it's all you!

Watch what goes into your precious vehicle.

Let's talk about one of your Sacred Spaces - **Your Reproductive System**

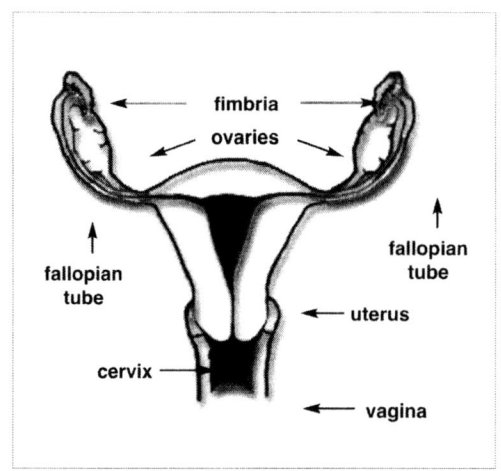

Ovaries - This is where not only your eggs are made, but also hormones that regulate your menstrual cycle. You have two (one on either side of your uterus.) During your cycle, one of your ovaries releases an egg, and if it becomes fertilized, your body begins to prepare for pregnancy.

Fimbria - Your Fimbria are at the end of your Fallopian tubes and hang right above your Ovaries. Their function is to draw the released eggs into your Fallopian tubes.

Fallopian Tubes - Your Fallopian Tubes look like two horns and sit on top of your uterus. They sort of work like an escalator, bringing your eggs down to your uterus from your ovaries.

Uterus - Your Uterus sits behind your bladder and is normally about the size of your fist. It is extremely strong and flexible. It houses and grows a fetus when a woman is pregnant and then pushes out the baby after nine months. The inside of your uterus is called the endometrium. It sheds and disintegrates every month, and the blood and fluids mixed together, create your menstrual cycle.

Cervix - Your Cervix is the entrance to your uterus. It sits at the top of your vagina. There is a tiny hole in the middle of it that lets out menstrual fluid and lets in sperm. Even though the opening is very small, if you have a baby, it opens wide enough to let the baby's head come through.

Vagina - Your Vagina is extremely flexible and connects the inside of your body with the outside of your body. It sits at an angle, leaning toward your back. It is made up of very strong muscles that can hold a tampon in place, accommodate a penis during sexual intercourse, and can stretch wide enough to let a baby pass through. Some people believe that your vagina is nasty and dirty, but actually it is really clean. It continuously sheds its cells and other fluids, (which is called a discharge). Your vaginal discharge will change from thinner to thicker during your monthly cycle - and this is completely normal. However, if you have a discharge that smells rotten, or is yellowish, greenish, lumpy or just doesn't look or feel right (remember, listen to your Intuition), you should see a doctor because you may have an infection.

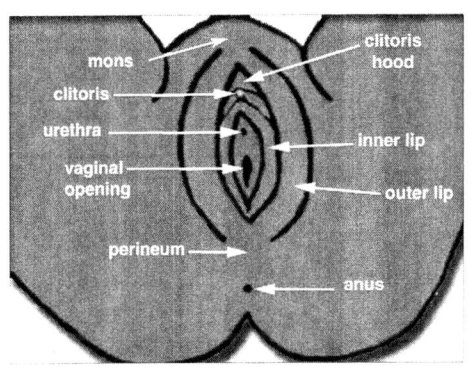

Mons - This is the protective layer of fat that sits on top of your pelvic bones (and is covered by pubic hair by the time you finish puberty).

Clitoris - The clitoris is a very sensitive little bundle of nerves (about the size of a pea) and is made entirely for your sexual pleasure.

Clitoris Hood - Because the clitoris is so sensitive, it is protected by a little hood, which keeps it from being stimulated all the time.

Urethra - This is where urine leaves your body. (It is the small hole that is just above the vaginal opening). Your urethra is a small tube that leads up to your bladder.

Outer Lips - Also called the labia majora (in medical terms). These are folds of skin that are covered with pubic hair and protect the inside of the vagina.

Inner Lips - Also called the labia minora (in medical terms). These are sensitive, hairless folds of membrane that act as another protection for the vagina.

Vaginal Opening - This is the entrance to the vagina (we talked about the vagina on the previous page).

Perineum - The area between your vagina and your anus.

Anus - The opening to your rectum. When you have a bowel movement, it comes from your intestines and leaves your body through your anus. (This part of your body was designed to be an "Exit" not an "Entrance.")

Don't forget, "You carry the seeds of the future" (in your body, mind and spirit)

There are many reasons why you want to protect your Sacred Reproductive System. It is the only one that you will receive, and as I mentioned earlier, your uterus is your primary creative center.

Your body is the home for the bundle of collective spiritual energy called "YOU." Just like a physical house that has many different rooms, your body is very similar and has many different rooms and energy centers. Your brain is your computer room or office, your heart area would be like your living room where you would entertain, meet, relax, love, laugh, dance and cry. Your uterus is your art room or creativity center. It is where most of your creative projects are developed and nurtured.

Many people in this society believe that the only function that your uterus has is to bear children. After a woman can no longer have children, or chooses not to have any, some people think that there is no use in her having a uterus. Because of this belief, many women decide to have hysterectomies (a surgical procedure to take out your uterus). Your uterus is so much, much more. It is one of those hidden sacred spaces inside of you. As I have already mentioned, its most popular function is of course, to house and grow a baby when a women gets pregnant - it's like a birthing center. But guess what? Through this Birthing Center, you can give birth to MORE than just physical babies, it is also where your "idea" and "dream" babies will be housed and grow. Your physical body and spiritual body are very connected. What happens in your physical house directly affects your spiritual well-being and your emotional state, and that in turn affects the health and well-being of your uterus (as well as other parts of your body).

Unfortunately, in this society, many women have not been able to express themselves creatively. They sometimes lack the money, necessary resources and emotional support to fully live out their life mission and dreams. When this happens, sometimes the uterus will get sick and become diseased. (Let me explain it a different way.) Just like in a regular house, when there is a fire, smoke or danger, usually, (in most houses) an alarm will go off. The alarm is loud and irritating to your ears because it is designed to alert you of danger. Your body house has a built-in alarm system as well - it's called PAIN. Physical and emotional pain is your house alarm system. Because we are spiritual beings, our physical body is designed to alert us when something is not the way it should be so that we can pay attention and take care of it before serious damage or injury occurs. When you have emotional pain that you have not dealt with, or ignored, it can set off the alarm system with physical pain.

Because many women are unable to nurture and care for their "idea" and "dream" babies, they die in the uterus. The good news is, that due to our tremendous Girl Power, "idea" and "dream" babies can still be born to a woman or girl who has had parts of her reproductive system damaged or removed. Your spirit is very resourceful. Ideally, it's great to be able to create in a room that is designed just for your creativity, however, sometimes you may have to be creative and use other parts of the house and create there. The wonderful thing about "idea" and "dream" babies, is that they enter the world differently than physical babies. Physical babies are nurtured and grow in the womb and pass through the vagina to enter the world. "Idea" and "dream" babies enter the world through your hands, your voice, your feet and your body in general.

Now that's Real Girl Power!

Are YOU nurturing your creativity?

Protecting my Sacred Spaces means protecting my future physical, "idea" and "dream" babies

Protecting Your Sacred Spaces

In an ideal world, you wouldn't need to protect yourself and your body. But unfortunately, that is not the world we live in. Many times we are born into situations that are not safe, and people that we are supposed to be safe with, create or allow us to be in unsafe situations. If you have ever experienced or are experiencing someone taking advantage of your body or doing things to you that your spirit doesn't feel comfortable with or good about, please tell an adult that you feel safe with.

A good way to tell if something is not right:
- It may feel good, but you feel ashamed or scared
- Someone tells you to keep it a secret
- It hurts

Rape and unwelcome touching are not about sex but about taking your Girl Power. If you have been raped, KNOW that it is about the other person's sickness and it's not your fault. No one should have to experience sexual abuse - whether you're 3, 13, or 30. No one should have to go through that because it's not okay for people to treat you like that - Period. It doesn't matter who it is - it's still not okay.

You may like or even love the person. And you may think that because you love them, they wouldn't do anything harmful to you. THIS IS NOT ABOUT LOVE! You may feel like or be told that it is your fault. The truth is - IT IS NOT! You are not responsible for ANYONE ELSE (especially adults). There are many people who will do harmful things to you, especially if they think that you are too scared, ashamed or confused to tell. You may think that things will get worse for you if you tell. It may not be easy, but find and tell a safe adult (a parent, teacher, friend, counselor, or mentor - just to name a few). Also, don't forget ALL of the people who are connected to you through your family tree. Pick someone you trust. Having the courage to tell, and not keeping it a secret is one of the BIGGEST ways to take back your Girl Power. It also gives the person who is harming you a chance to get help and not hurt anyone else in this way.

Help For Protecting Your Sacred Spaces

Your Sacred Space is where your inner child and creativity live. And you'll need both your inner child and creativity for the rest of your life. Protecting your Sacred Spaces may require you to get an internal watchdog.

(I'll let you in on a little secret - the Creator knew you would need one, so you have a built-in watchdog. It's named your Intuition and it hangs out around your stomach area or your gut.)

Intuition is just like having your very own personal guard dog. However, don't be fooled, Intuition is not some fancy poodle - this is a SERIOUS guard dog whose main job is to protect you and to look out for your best interest. It can hear and see things that you can't (just like a real dog) and its ears perk up when danger is lurking.

Just like a physical guard dog, Intuition requires you to spend time with it for you to build up trust in its ability to protect you. But know that Intuition is as real as any Pit Bull or Rottweiler. It doesn't play. When you are in danger, or something doesn't look, feel or smell right, Intuition will let you know. How? You'll feel it rumbling around in the pit of your stomach or it'll cause your heart to start beating fast (its way of barking and getting your attention).

Create a new relationship with your body through talking to your watchdog "Intuition" - Asking it "What does this mean?" "What should I do?" If you listen carefully (and don't panic), you will know what the best solution is - even if it means to go and ask someone else for help. If there is a way out, or if you just need to get through something, make sure you listen to Intuition because it is always on the job.

Your body carries many memories and emotions. Many girls walk around not attached to their bodies. Oftentimes because our girl power has been taken away from us in some way - we leave, or "check out."

We space out, vacate the building. When this happens, it becomes difficult for us to hear Intuition. (If this has happened or is happening to you, it's very important that you seek help so that you can work through it.)

Know that Intuition is very faithful and loyal to you no matter what. Trust your Intuition. Intuition can't always stop things from happening to you, but listening to Intuition (as soon as you hear it beginning to bark) can head off and sometimes even prevent dangerous situations from even occurring.

A gift from the Creator

Ready, willing and able to serve and protect YOU!

*Have you ever felt lonely even while
people were around?*

*Have you ever felt like life was a 10-ton weight
holding you down?& no matter how you fight to survive
it's as if it's a struggle just to make it through alive.*

*Have you ever felt tired after sleep?
Your body felt so beaten, tired and weak
that you couldn't go on.
Like someone had stolen your soul.*

*I lost my soul so long ago,
to be honest,
I don't want it anymore.*

*- Melanie Davis
(age 15)*

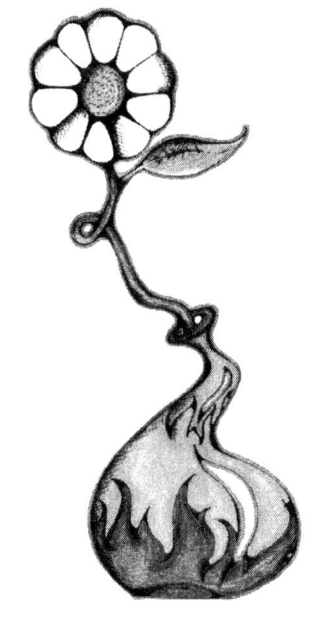

— *Chapter 7* —
"Why Do I Sometimes Feel Like I'm Going Crazy?"

Periods, Mood Swings and the Moon

Periods. There are many things that I could share with you about periods. In African culture, beginning your cycle was a magical time that marked the beginning of your rites of passage to womanhood. During a young girl's "Rites of Passage", she (along with other girls her age) would go to a special place (away from the men and boys), and be taught by women about their bodies and all the things that are important about being a woman.

In this culture, periods are not talked about nearly enough. Unfortunately, most times our mothers never completely understood them, probably because their mothers didn't talk about it. (Believe it or not, your grandmother and her mother may not have even known what their period was when it started because no one ever explained it.). Even though our menstrual cycle is something that we share with other women, many of us are still embarrassed to even buy pads and tampons in a store. I'm not really sure why this is so uncomfortable. Maybe it's because even though we have not been taught a lot about our cycles, we have picked up on the idea of feeling a little bit dirty and ashamed about it.

I know when I first started having my cycle, I would dread standing in line at a store with my "monthly" products (especially if there was a male in the line either in front or behind me. I would purposely get in the line with the female clerk.) It's like we have an unspoken rule that we should keep it a secret. A secret that everybody knows, but no one feels comfortable talking about. (Maybe it is because we typically don't go through a formal Rites of Passage in this country.)

Most of the information that you know or have heard about your period, focuses on the physical changes that happen in your body (and that's very important stuff to know and understand). However, what you may not hear too much about are the spiritual and creative changes that happen along with your period every month. (That is what we're going to talk the most about.)

As I mentioned earlier, you have a very special and unique relationship with the Moon. Your menstrual cycle is directly connected to the cycles of the moon. Understanding how your menstrual cycle is closely linked to the moon will not only give you some much needed information about how your body works, but also why you can have so many different moods each month. Through our monthly cycles, we are linked to all the other women on the planet that are still having their monthly periods, as well as to the moon (which the earth cycles around each month).

Most girls experience their first menstrual period between the ages of 9 and 15. This marks the beginning of a wonderfully magical part of your journey until you become around the age of 45 or so (unless you become pregnant or suffer the loss of your period due to other physical circumstances). When and if this happens, you still have a strong relationship to the moon - it just shifts and you get to experience the moon in a different way.

Each month, your body will go through a series of changes (many of them will repeat themselves every 28 days or so). These are changes that may affect your weight, heart rate, breast size and tenderness, your vaginal discharge , your concentration, your vision and hearing, your nerves, your psychic ability and Intuition. Understanding how your body reacts to your cycle will help you to gain control and balance in your life.

Cycles of the Moon and Our Bodies

The Moon (just like your body) has its own cycle. A full cycle of the moon lasts for almost 30 days. It is consistent and very predictable, which is why it was one of the very first ways that we began measuring time - in months. Let's look at how our cycles are connected to the Moon's cycles...

Dark or New Moon During this phase, the bright face of the moon is turned away from the earth. Most women and girls menstruate during this or the Full Moon phase.

When your period comes, it actually marks the end of your cycle. Your body is releasing the egg from the previous month. Just as the moon withdraws its light from the earth, many women, find that during the actual bleeding or menstruation phase, we tend to want to withdraw our energies from the outer world - turning inward. As you naturally turn inward, you become very sensitive and your Intuition is wide awake. You may become more tired and want to sleep more (your body is loosing blood, so it's natural to not have energy to do a lot of extra activities). You may find that you want to stay home and organize your closet, write some poetry, draw, or just chill with a good book or a crossword puzzle.

This is a time for you to listen to your inner voice. Journal, take warm baths, spend time in quiet reflection with you as much as you can. (Now I know that life doesn't just stop because you are menstruating. You still have to go to work or school.) Charting your cycle on a calendar can be an important tool because it will allow you to know when the "bleeding" part of your cycle will begin. This can help you to plan to slow things down.

I have been charting my cycle for years and I have it down to the exact day (every 26 days.) My period always starts in the mornings. Because I know the day and time I generally start, I try to slow my schedule down during that time. I try not to make a lot of plans with other people because I really just want to be by myself. I usually don't feel like doing a lot of talking. If I have to be around a lot of people during my cycle, I can seem unsocial and moody.

This phase of your cycle marks the end of the past month. It is a good time to reflect. As your body is releasing the old egg, take time to release old emotions, thoughts, feelings and patterns that no longer serve you. It is a good time to release tears. Don't judge yourself too harshly.
LOVE YOURSELF THROUGH RELEASE.

Waxing or Crescent Moon During this phase, the moon is expanding and gaining in energy. This is the time right after your period. Because your uterus has just released an egg, this is a wonderful time of renewal, giving you an excellent opportunity to gain in strength, self-love and confidence. Just as the moon is being reborn again, this is typically a time when you will feel alive, energetic and enthusiastic. During this phase of your cycle, because you are feeling renewed and fresh, new inspirations have room to grow. Your energies are beginning to turn outward and you want to have fun and once again be around other people. Take time out to play, get some exercise, enjoy your friends, laugh, be silly and childlike (which will be easy to do during this time of the month - as even the moon is playfully peeking through the darkness).

Have you ever noticed how young children can sometimes be very honest? They will tell you if something looks funny or strange to them. They tell the truth (even if it may hurt your feelings). They ask all kinds of questions because they are not old enough to know that it is not "polite" to ask such things. Well, this is a time when you are child-like in your cycle and you may find yourself not pretending to like something (when you really don't). If you hookup with "Intuition" and listen to what it has to say, you may find yourself speaking your mind.

This phase marks the beginning of a new cycle, new beginnings and new ideas.
BE HAPPY, CONFIDENT, EMPOWERED AND STRONG AS YOU STEP OUT INTO THE WORLD!

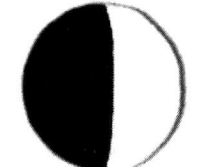

Half Moon During this phase, just as the moon is continuing to grow in brightness and energy, this is typically your preovulation phase. What I mean by "preovulation" is that your ovaries are preparing to release an egg. You may find yourself growing in energy and feeling excited about life. This is typically the time of the month when you are not feeling as needy emotionally because you are growing in energy from the inside out. Life feels good and you can accomplish more at school or work by using that extra inner drive to concentrate and work toward completing your goals. Still feeling confident and creative, see and experience yourself connecting to the bigger picture of life.

LET YOUR "MOON" LIGHT SHINE FOR ALL THE WORLD TO SEE!

Full Moon During this phase of the moon, most women and girls either start their periods or ovulate (it is more common to ovulate during this time). "Ovulation" is the time of the month when one of your ovaries releases an egg. Just as the moon is full of energy and it is at its brightest, our bodies become full of light and energy and we can become extremely attractive to boys and men during this phase. (This is typically the time of the month when you are sexually very vulnerable because your natural sex drive can be high.) Your spirit is ready to give birth to something. You may feel more loving and affectionate toward others and if you add that to an increase in your sexual energy - you may find yourself extremely vulnerable! Remember, your Girl Power is pretty strong anyway, but especially during this time of the month. You may find yourself dressing a little bit more sexy (when you are ovulating) to get attention - so just be aware of the energy that you are naturally sending out. (It's nothing to feel ashamed of, but you have to make sure that you find a balance. Many unplanned pregnancies happen because girls and women don't understand what is happening within them.) You may all of a sudden feel really strong urges to have a baby and/or you may find that you want to take care of others - in a motherly kind of way. This is perfectly natural, but know that your body vehicle doesn't know whether you are emotionally, financially and spiritually ready to have a child - it's just doing it's job.

Let me explain it this way, the Creator has set up your body vehicle in such a way that mostly all of your internal functions are programmed to occur automatically. Unless something is physically wrong with you, you normally don't have to think about breathing. It happens automatically. It's the same with all of your internal organs: your heart, your bladder, your lungs, your liver and so on. Everything is set to function without little input from you, including your reproductive system. You neither create nor release the eggs in your body. Your body vehicle is just doing what it is programmed to do. What you DO control, is how and where you drive your vehicle (as well as who you invite in.) Your body is not in control - you are. You are the driver. But just be aware that you are giving off a lot of powerful attractive energy when you ovulate. Your body vehicle's system is set up to release an egg to create another human being. Men and boys (with the help of their body vehicles) will be attracted to you (not just because you are the wonderful person that you are) but because their bodies are constantly producing sperm whose only job is to fertilize women and girls eggs. Their bodies are designed to be ready for action almost anytime of the month. (We'll talk more about them later.)

If you pay attention to you, you can use this time of the month to give more of your powerful Full Moon energy to your "idea" and "dream" babies. Just like your sexual energy, your creative energy is strong when you ovulate as well. Pay attention to your dreams and listen to your friend and companion "Intuition." Use your natural Full Moon energy to let your family and loved ones know how much you appreciate them. Do something physical like exercising (aerobics, kickboxing, running, dancing, skating - anything to help burn off some of that excess energy). Use your extra strength and wisdom to help others. If the urge to have a baby is strong, spend some time around young children (this can be a good time to make some extra money baby-sitting, because your Motherly energy is at its peak.)

Make it a point to share some of that powerful Full Moon energy with yourself. Show yourself some love. Use your creative energy to produce something physical: write a children's story, paint, draw, make music, write a song - be creative.

USE THE LIGHT OF THE FULL MOON TO SHOW THE DIVINE LIGHT WITHIN YOU

Waning or Crescent Moon During this phase, the egg is released, and if it was not fertilized, it is commonly known as your Premenstrual phase. Your sexual energy is still very high, but it is beginning to decrease, and you once again begin to slowly turn more inward. You may feel more restless and aggressive (partly because you physically have an egg inside of you that didn't get fertilized). You may feel angry, frustrated, guilty and depressed and not know why. You still have a lot of sexual energy, but because it is shifting, if you are not careful, it can be really destructive. Your energy can change from motherly to seductive. This can be destructive because you may participate in more risky behavior and even lack a sense of responsibility. You may find that you have more of a desire to sexually tease males or act out during this time because you still feel powerful. You may give off loving energy one moment and then angry, aggressive, demanding energy the next (I mean even ready to fight.) From the outside you can seem "straight up CRAZY" (but you and I both know that you are not). You may notice that you are less concerned about hurting other people's feelings, and because you can't physically lash out, you may lash out with your tongue - saying what you feel and sometimes being just "plain ole" mean.

While your body is shifting, your breasts and belly may begin to swell, your weight may change, you may find that it is harder to concentrate. Your emotions are up and down, you are restless, sensitive and very moody. Use it to your advantage.

This is a good time to use your Third Eye and your creative visualization skills to decide what changes need to be made in your life. You can use all of that destructive energy to clear away the old and unwanted in your life. This is typically the time when you want to make major changes (whether in habits, relationships, hairstyles - any and everything). Your body is about to release the old egg from the previous month. Use this time to once again spend less time interacting with others and more time with you, realizing that you have to release the old in order to make room for the new.

Bless the egg that didn't get fertilized. Use your Third Eye to visualize it being released from your body without any judgment from you. If it is at all possible, make some time to be with yourself. Really use the Chapter called, "Creating Sacred Spaces." Decide to make a change in your life, however small.

LOOK TOWARD THE LIGHT OF THE NEW MOON AS YOU ONCE AGAIN PASS FROM RELEASING THE OLD INTO THE NEW.

I have gone rather quickly through the major changes in the Moon and our menstrual cycle. I just highlighted the big changes. Just know, that each and every day your energy is changing like the Moon - it is a gradual process. Every day that you have an opportunity, look up and check out the Moon. See what it is doing, then focus on what is happening inside of you.

Connecting with the moon's monthly cycles connects you with Mother Earth, other women and the Universe.

Just as the moon changes from new to full then back to dark again, life is ever-changing: growing, transforming, and dying - only to be reborn, over and over again.

Depression, Anger and Sadness

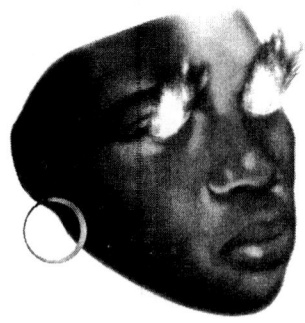

There are many things that are going to happen to you throughout your life. Some are designed to teach you valuable lessons. Some you may never fully understand. Stress is a natural part of being human. It teaches us how to make healthy choices, create boundaries, and build character (just to name a few). Our body vehicle is just like any other vehicle - it gets worn down over time (especially if you don't take care of it). It is very important that you tune in to what is happening inside of you and have the courage to make changes or seek help when you need to.

Let's say that you were driving in your car, and the red light on the dashboard began flashing to let you know that you need to check your brakes. What if you ignored it and just kept on driving? Then, the oil light came on, and you just kept on driving. Finally, the gas light began flashing and you ignored that, too. What would happen? Either your brakes would go out and you would not be able to control the vehicle, you would have no oil (which could really mess up your engine), or you would run out of gas. Can you imagine if all three happened at the same time? You would really be in trouble. Well, our bodies give us warning lights too. What are some of them?

- your appetite may change (you either want a lot more food or a lot less food)

- you don't have any energy and you feel sad

- you can't sleep or you wake up in the middle of the night and can't get back to sleep

- you are angry and you keep it on the inside

- you get a bad case of acne and other bumps and knots show up on your skin

- your hair starts falling out when you comb it

- you want to hurt yourself (like carving into your skin and doing other destructive things to your body)

- you want to do drugs and/or alcohol

- you feel worthless and believe that nobody cares about you

- you give other people permission to do harmful things to your body

- you think about your death a lot and/or committing suicide

- you say all kinds of mean and cruel things to yourself inside of your head

- you want to just scream! (but you don't)

All of these things are Warning Lights on our dashboards that let us know that something is wrong.

Anger is not a bad thing. (In fact, there are a lot of things that we SHOULD be angry about.) Anger is one of the warning lights that the Creator has given us. Anger will let you know when it is necessary for you to create stronger boundaries and check to see what's happening inside. Many times we get angry because we feel powerless. But we have to deal with it, or it will take over.

Sadness is like anger (but just turned inside). You may have lost something or someone that you needed or wanted. As a human being, you need to feel good about who you are as a person. Sadness can let you know when you need support. Take time out to get support, to grieve and to figure out different ways to meet your needs.

Our emotions carry energy - and energy cannot be destroyed, only changed. When, for example, you are angry with someone, and don't let it go or deal with it - you wind up stuffing it. Literally compacting it down and squeezing it into some part of your body vehicle. You have to deal with it because, sooner or later (sometimes even many years later), that stuffed up anger will create problems or situations that may be a lot harder for you to ignore - the WARNING LIGHTS are called "Drama" and "Pain." Drama can happen in many ways when problems aren't dealt with effectively. Sometimes we may think that we are angry. And that may be true, but sometimes we can act angry and really be sad or even scared. Other people can create "Drama" for us as well. Whatever you are feeling - know that it is real and valid simply because you are experiencing it.

Can you think of ways that "Drama" shows up in your life? What were the first warning signs?

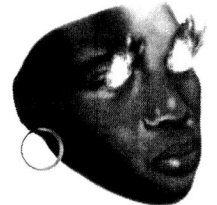

**The most important conversations that
you will ever have are with yourself.**

If you are feeling angry, sad or depressed, and you KNOW that there are things happening to you that you haven't completely dealt with (like someone taking advantage of your body, someone threatening you, or anything), PLEASE GET SOME SUPPORT. It is so very important to learn to speak up and out.

Talking and/or writing out your problems is a wonderful tool. It is a way of moving that energy instead of stuffing it in your body only to later look in the mirror and realize that it is trying to escape through the pores on your face in the form of a great big zit, weight loss or gain, drug use, and a whole lot of other painful stuff.

**Even if life were a rose garden,
you would still have to put up with the thorns.**

Meditation and the Mothership

The best ways that I know of to help deal with stress, are to make sure that I am getting enough rest and nutrition, and to Meditate. What is Meditation? For me, it simply means taking time to be alone, focus on my breathing and then listening. (Look back at the Chapter on "Creating Sacred Spaces.")

Sometimes when I meditate, I sit comfortably, and once I have tuned my internal radio to the Divine frequency, I quiet my body. Thoughts run through my head - but I don't try to hold on to them. When I am calm, relaxed and open, I imagine that my body is surrounded in a bright white light. And as my body fills with light, I become lighter and lighter. I am like a space ship floating out in the middle of the Universe. There is a door at the very top of my head. I slowly open it. I can see the long (almost invisible) cords that connect me to a much bigger ship (I call it the Mothership). I know that it contains the Creator and everyone that I care about, and everyone that cares about me in the Spirit World. I am completely unafraid. Sometimes, I ask questions, but mostly, I just listen. When I am done, (there is no time limit) I slowly come back down to earth. When I meditate, I am reminded that I am NEVER alone and that I am supported. (YOU are NEVER alone and you do have support.) Whenever I feel stressed and depressed, I hook up to the Mothership and get refueled.

This is just one way of doing it. Try it, or use your imagination to come up with something that works for you. The most important thing is to Make the CONNECTION.

Go for the all-important goal of loving yourself (fully and completely). Start by simply looking in the mirror and smiling at YOU. Over time, when you are ready, look in the mirror and say, "I like YOU." Eventually, work your way up to "I love and respect YOU." (See how much self-love you can stand.)

**The one thing that we
can always change is our Attitude.**

*To change is to grow.
To change often means to grow much.*

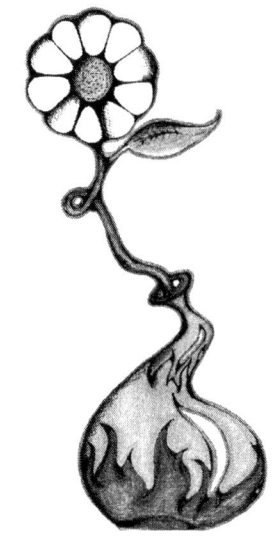

— Chapter 8 —

"Taking Care of My Body"

Food and My Mood

In addition to the influences of the Moon on our personality, there is another very strong factor: the food that we eat - what we choose to put inside our vehicle. Food is fuel. When you eat food, your body changes it into something that it can use. All nutritious foods contain water - and the water makes it easier to move food through our body system, and you eliminate (through your colon) whatever is not useful to your body.

Many times we literally put "junk in our trunk" with the food choices that we make. We need nutritious food to strengthen our bodies, and eating junk can be like putting sugar in the gas tank of our vehicle. Not only can it affect how we feel, but also it can affect our energy level, our ability to concentrate and sleep. The crazy thing about junk food is that it is very addictive. The more you eat, your body will begin to crave it. It can be like a drug. It gets your body vehicle all off track. Your body can't find very much nutrition in junk food, so it winds up getting stopped up in our colon and clogs up other parts of your body.

Choose foods that will serve your body and your life's mission.

During your monthly cycle, exercise and the foods you eat can affect your mood and add to PMS and the pain of cramps.
Foods to avoid: Chocolate, sugar, salt, caffeine...
Foods to eat: Bananas, soups, grains, herbal teas, vegetables and of course, drink lots, and lots of Water...

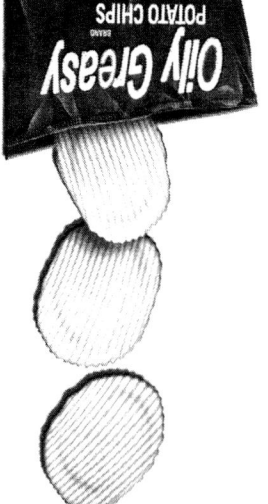

What Do We Really Need from Food Anyway?

Your body needs food for two main reasons:
- as fuel for your body vehicle
- as maintenance to keep your body functioning at its very best

We get energy from the foods that we eat (just like a car needs gas in order to run). When you eat food it is broken down into usable forms in your stomach and intestines and it is then transported throughout your body via your bloodstream.

What Gives Us the Most Juice (energy)?

The Sun
Our most powerful source of energy is the sun.

Fruits, Veggies and Grains
Vegetables are able to change the energy that comes directly from the sun into a way that our bodies can easily use.

Vegetarians
Animals (including humans) don't get our food energy directly from the sun, we have to get it from fruits, vegetables and grains. Our bodies are designed to take in energy in this secondhand way.

Meat Eaters (includes animals and humans) Now the energy of the sun has to go through the Fruits, Veggies and Grains and then through the Vegetarian animals and then finally to the animals and humans that eat other animals for food. The sun energy isn't as strong because of all that it has had to go through to get to you.

Is Pork - Black Folks Meat?

Why do we eat the foods that we do? When you think of Asian people, what foods come to mind? Probably Chinese food or Thai food. What about Italian? Do you think about spaghetti or pizza?

What foods come to mind for African-Americans? Soul food, right? **Where did Soul food come from?**

When our ancestors were forced through slavery to come here from Africa, they didn't come with care packages and lunch boxes. They were unable to bring the spices and foods they used in Africa. Because of the conditions of slavery, they were forced to eat things in order to survive. They lived on plantations, and grew mostly all of the food that they would eat. Because they were enslaved, even though they raised many animals for food, they were unable to keep and eat the best parts. Let's use the pig for example. Because slave owners knew that pigs loved to eat garbage and lay around in the mud, they only ate certain parts. The rest of the pig would be left for the slaves to eat. Our great, great grandmothers were so creative and smart, in order for their families to survive, they used what they had to make meals for their families. They didn't have any choices. It was either eat the leftover pig parts or starve (hopefully you have never been faced with starvation - if you have, you know that it is like life or death - if you get hungry enough, you will eat anything). They had to eat, because they still had to work - they were enslaved and didn't have the choices that we have today.

Getting back to the pig. The parts of the pig that the slave owners and their families didn't want, they gave to the slaves (always keeping the very best for themselves.) Our great, great grandmothers, used their creativity to keep their families from starving. Practically every part was cooked up and served. Very little was thrown away. Now, because our great, great grandmothers were awesome, they were able to make even the feet and intestines of a pig taste good. Because they were so creative and were good at any and everything they did, they fed their families. They also remembered some of the plants that they had back in Africa. They were very smart.

For many, many, many years, only the foods that were not really the best for our bodies were available, so, we not only grew used to eating them, but we liked them too (remember, our great, great grandmothers were excellent cooks). They were able to be very creative in cooking up a pig. They made cooking oil or grease out of the pig (lard), chitlins (the stomach and intestines), the feet, tail ears, legs - everything was used. Everything but the "Oink" of a pig was used to keep their families alive.

Give thanks for our ancestors!

Because of their creativity, resourcefulness and willingness to do what it took to stay alive, we are able to be here today. Today, black people are culturally identified with the same foods that our great, great, great grandparents had to eat. They taught their children what they knew and they taught their children the same. And some people today think that if we don't eat the way our great, great, great grandmothers taught us, we are saying that what they taught us was not good enough. That is completely not true. Mostly all of us live in cities today and the animals that we eat aren't cared for like the animals that our ancestors ate. Pigs, cows and even chickens were raised on farms eating natural things. 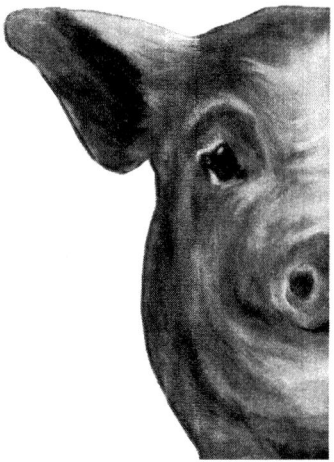 Today, many are raised in factories and plants (instead of out in the sunshine with grass and fresh air) and are given drugs to make them grow bigger faster. The bad part is that all of the drugs and unnatural things that go into the animals bodies, also go into our bodies when we eat them.

Because we have eaten foods that aren't the best for our bodies, many Black people suffer more from diseases like high blood pressure, and diabetes. You don't have to eliminate meat from your diet completely, but do watch what you eat (especially red meat - pork and beef).

Honor your Ancestors by choosing foods that strengthen your body, mind and spirit.

*H*ygiene

Why is hygiene so important? It's maintenance for the vehicle you get to use while you are here on the planet (your mobile home.) You have to take care of it because you can't trade it in.

Washing your hands with soap and water for example, is important because germs are often transported from one location to another through your hands.

Let's say you wake up, look in the mirror and discover that three big white pus-filled bumps have invaded your face overnight. What should you do?

First of all, don't keep touching it! The skin on your face is usually more sensitive than the skin on other parts of your body. Remember, your hands carry germs that you pick up from everywhere (door-knobs, books, touching other people, animals and things - just to name a few). You won't be able to see the germs, but know that they are there! Every time you touch your face (which includes your eyes, nose, ears and mouth) and haven't washed your hands, you increase the chances of not only spreading germs but also getting sick. A lot of colds are spread by people not washing their hands and then touching their mouths or eyes.

Remember that your body is your vehicle and the only way that it can sometimes let you know when something is wrong, out of balance or needs your attention is to give you a warning signal. (And unfortunately, sometimes warning signals come in the form of pimples.) Before you decide to try to cover them up with makeup, ask your body what this means. What is the message?

Your body could be trying to tell you something simple like, "drink more water" so that it can flush all the things that it doesn't need out. It could be saying, "you need to change the products you use on your face", or that "you are really stressed out and need to deal with ____." Your body could also be trying to let you know that "you need to add or eliminate certain things from your diet." Pay attention to your body and learn to listen. It could also be trying to tell you to simply "remember to wash your hands more - especially before touching your face."

Our bodies are different in that we each have our own special way of communicating with ourselves. You have your own special system, so pay attention to you, and don't forget to listen to Intuition. Your face is just one part of the skin that you are in. Many times we spend the most time taking care of our faces. Well, the rest of your body needs just as much attention, love and support from you.

It doesn't have to cost a lot of money to make sure that your body is washed (every part) on a daily basis. Your skin is alive and is constantly shedding old dead cells to make room for new ones. That is why it is so important to make sure that you wash every part of your body (with the exception of your hair) every day.

> Nurturing your body not only helps you to remember how precious you are, but it helps others to remember too - when they see your example of how to take care of you.

Practice Pampering

As you get older and your life gets busier, you may find it a little harder to always remember to really take care of you. Many people are going to want your precious time. Sometimes women forget to pamper and nurture themselves for long periods of time. Neglecting yourself will definitely create stress and it could cause you to begin to feel drab and uninspired. And when you feel bad about you on the inside, it will show on the outside.

Begin a habit of doing something special for your body each and every day. Especially on the days when you are feeling really "blah!" It could be something as small as putting extra lotion on your feet and elbows (even if no one will see them but you). Take bubble baths, give yourself a facial, polish your toenails. Do whatever you need to do to communicate love and respect for your body temple.

Find your balance between taking care of your inner and outer worlds.

— Chapter 9 —

"What's Wrong with My Hair, and Why Won't It Grow?"

Me and My Hair

Hair. When it's looking good we feel confident, sassy and beautiful, but when it's looking bad - there are few things worse than having a really bad hair day.

Our hair has always been a challenge to work with and understand. From the time we arrive on the planet, our families and loved ones will watch to see if that "beautiful, shiny, soft, curly" head of hair that many black babies are born with, will turn BAD. We learn at a very young age that people think that there is something wrong with the way the Creator designed us - because our hair has to be "fixed" soon after we arrive.

The real deal is, (listen closely) **THERE IS NOTHING WRONG WITH YOUR NATURAL HAIR.** The problem is that for many many years, because our hair is so different in texture from other cultures - no one else really understood it. And because WE never really understood it either - the natural condition of our hair became (and still is for some) a source of shame and embarrassment.

Our thick, springy, kinky, wool-like in texture hair, is really one of the most awesome gifts that we have from the Creator. It can be one of the greatest expressions of our creativity. No other culture's hair has the versatility of Black hair. You can change your entire look anytime you choose. It is uniquely YOU. Even if you are in a family and all of the children have the same parents, your hair can look, act and feel different from your mother's, your sister's, your father's and your brother's. Why? Because your hair is a living organ just like your skin, teeth and nails. The natural wave pattern of your hair is uniquely yours - it's like your fingerprint. No one else has your hair. And because, our hair is like our fingerprint (with no two exactly alike) it is a challenge to find products and services that work well for ALL black folk's hair. Even on your head, your hair may be soft in the front, thick and springy in the middle and really kinky in the back. It is uniquely you. Understanding and establishing a loving, lifelong relationship with your hair - is not always going to be easy.

Remember, your body is the unique vehicle that you get to use while you are here. The more you take time out to listen to and understand your vehicle (and that includes your hair) the more rewarding your experience will be. Your hair has a language all its own, and your job is to figure it out yourself, or pay a professional hair stylist to do it.

How much do you really know about your hair?

Your hair gets its nourishment from the foods you eat and the water you drink. Its condition can be negatively affected if you smoke cigarettes, eat a lot of salt, drink a lot of alcohol, don't get enough sleep, as well as doing all kinds of not so nice things to it.

I've heard women say that they don't want to wear their hair natural or "lock" it because they don't want to be locked into any one style. Perms put you in bondage and lock you up in a different way. Relaxed hair is permanently changed. Chemicals remove the hair's natural protective coating and that is one reason why it is weaker than hair that hasn't been processed. For permanent relaxers, professional stylists are the best way to go. If you decide to do it yourself, make sure that you don't over-process your hair by re-perming hair that has already been permed. And make sure that you completely rinse all chemicals from your hair.

Your hair in its natural state, can give you many creative options. Before you decide to "permanently" alter your hair, take the time to get to know it. You may be surprised.

You can fight with it, burn it, relax it, color it, shave it, straighten it, cut it, braid it, press it, lock it, tease it, overheat it, wrap it, bleach it, roll it, twist it or weave it. But guess what?
You still have to deal with it.
It will still affect how you feel as a girl or a woman.
You might as well learn how to live with it, understand it, celebrate it and love it.

The Hair Test

How much do you really know about YOUR hair? What is your natural hair really like? Before your next perm, weave, curl or extensions, spend a few moments getting to know your hair. (I know you are probably saying "I already KNOW my hair - it's NAPPY!") Well, there is much more to it...

      1. Take a look at your hair in the mirror. Are the roots naturally curly, wavy, straight or tightly coiled?

      2. Does it look really dry, normal or oily?

      3. If you were to take a strand of your hair between your fingers, does your hair feel: slightly rigid? (then it's 'porous'), flat and smooth? (then it's 'non-porous'), or is it rough and rigid? (then it's 'overly porous')

      4. Is your hair naturally thick, medium or thin?

      5. If you were to pull one single strand of your hair from the root, would it stretch without breaking? (it has elasticity). If it stretches a little and then breaks (it has a little elasticity). And if it breaks really easily (it has no elasticity).

After you test your hair, make an appointment to have a hair consultation with a good hair care professional. You DON'T have to commit to having your hair styled, just see if they give you the same information about your hair. The more you know about your hair, the better you can care for it by choosing products that are better suited to fit you.

My Personal Hair-Story

My earliest memories of my hair, begin with my mother using hair grease and water to fix my hair. It was strong and kinky. The older I got the thicker it got. I remember many a day sitting in front of the stove getting my hair pressed with the hot comb. This was particularly challenging during the hot, muggy summers in Chicago. My mother would always start the pressing sessions with the back of my head and work her way to the front. Many days, the weather would be so hot and humid that by the time she got almost to the front, my "kitchens" (that's what we used to call the hair near the bottom of your neck) would begin napping up. It was quite a battle.

As I got older, I began styling my own hair. I could never get the hang of using pressing combs and curling irons. I had many battle scars to prove it. Burns on my forehead, my ears, and my neck. In many of my photos I noticed that I had bangs (probably in part to hide the burns on my forehead).

I first got introduced to "perms" at home, once again, sitting in the kitchen. I endured my scalp burning, in an attempt to leave the chemicals on longer so that my naturally course hair would become straight. What I didn't like with perms, was that they were permanent. Once my hair was chemically straightened, it was thinner and weaker, and a lot easier to break off and split. I quickly learned that chemicals are best in the hands of professionals and that it was important to find someone with whom I trusted. It was a very expensive and time-consuming process. Finding and keeping a good stylist was a challenge. When I would find someone that I thought was good, she (or he) would overbook appointments and I would spend an entire afternoon waiting to get my hair done. They or I would move. And sometimes I just didn't have the money. Some of my "best" hair styles were only temporary. My hair would grow and each time it would look different.

When I was a college student with limited funds, my hair became really damaged. I was away at a predominantly white school, and there were no black salons in the area. Out of desperation, I allowed another student (who was in the same dilemma), to do my hair. It was disastrous. My hair became very damaged and brittle. I soon realized that the relationship that I had with my hair was very personal. I had to find what worked for me.

I began really studying my hair. I tried a jheri curl, and with it, my hair grew really long. But I didn't like the drippy look (thus, I avoided all cameras). As I let my natural hair grow out, I wore braids and cornrows. When I finally took the braids out, I looked at the abundance of hair that was mine. I realized that what my hair wanted all along was moisture and a break from the heat appliances and chemicals. I came out of chemical perms about 12 years ago when I ended a career as a Flight Attendant. I found that I didn't really need a perm. I began to use my creativity and experiment with different products. When I saw a woman that I judged had a similar grade of hair to mine and I liked the way it looked, I would ask her what she was using. I learned a lot about my hair (both good and bad).

For me, my hair is a representation and a reflection of the relationship that I am having with myself. When I look at old pictures of myself, I remember my life's struggles and accomplishments. Pictures remind me that everything is temporal and changing (even the perfect "do").

> **My hair broadcasts to the world the relationship I am having with myself.**

About six years ago, I went through a major transition again in my life. On the inside I was different. As a result, I needed a new look, so I shaved my head. It marked the beginning of a new phase of self-discovery. It was the first time in my life that I could get in the shower or a pool and not have a plastic cap on my head. It was powerful. I felt empowered. I realized that my hair was a wonderful accessory, but that with or without it, I was still me. I grew in self-confidence, cultural pride and love. After another personal growth spurt, I decided to let my hair grow out naturally. As my "baby locs" grew, I made sure that they were well-groomed, healthy and loved.

Having natural hair is another way that I have found to nurture myself. I enjoy the feel of my hair and the relationship that my hair and I are cultivating. I'm on a life-long journey with my hair. I've learned to not be so mean to it. To not punish it for needing lots of moisture and water. I listen to my hair (it's like my "spiritual antennas"). I feed it when it's hungry, I protect it from cigarette smoke and harsh weather with head wraps and scarfs, and I'm patient with it when it's having a "bad" hair day.

Are locks the end of the road for me? Have I arrived at the last stop on the hairstyle train? No. I try not to get too attached to any particular style or "look" because I realize that it's all temporary. I am ever- growing and changing. Changing my hair is an unspoken way of letting the world know that something different is happening in me. My hair teaches me that I have choices, freedom and versatility each and every day. It teaches me that life is a journey. I give thanks for my hair and all that it has taught me. I'll take pictures to remember this phase and when it is time to transform into something new and different - I will.

Who knows what my next look will be (one thing I know - it won't be anything permanent) - (written in 2002)

Wherever you are in your hair care journey, know that it is lifelong, so be patient. Your hair can be a wonderful way to express your creativity, style, mood and all the exciting things that are uniquely you.

Do you Have Good Hair?

<u>New Definition</u>
- Is your hair healthy?
- Is it clean and well-groomed?
- Is it reflecting the inner beauty of the person that it is attached to?

If it is - then that's some "Good Hair!"

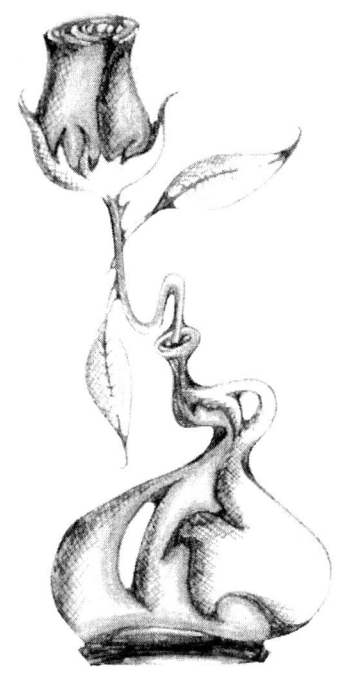

— *Chapter 10* —
*I*nfluences of the *M*edia

"Lights, Camera, Action. Sorry Ms. Jackson..."
(It's not for real)

Magazines and television are designed to sell you something: an idea, a product or a lifestyle. Let's talk about T.V. for a minute. What do shows like, Jerry Springer and Flavor of Love have in common? Most of the shows are pretty much based on SEX. Watching shows like this can give you the impression that "EVERYBODY" thinks the way that the show's participants do. For example, they try to make you believe that everybody is sleeping around or trying to get people to sleep with them. That is not the truth. Some people will do or say just about anything to get on television. You never see what happens after the show. But what do you think happens after **"lights, camera, action?"**

Music, the Media and My Mind

Every moment of the day, there is a contest going on. The television, movie and music industries are competing for your precious: time, energy, money and brain - nonstop. You have to really (and I mean REALLY) pay close attention to what you watch, listen and respond to. One reason is that your internal computer center (your brain) records every image you see and every word you hear. It stores everything you come in contact with. Most times you will not even be aware of your brain recording  (because it is one of those automatic functions that the Creator has placed in your body vehicle).

Your internal computer system has several different functions. You have a part called your "Conscious Mind", and it is the part of your brain that you make decisions and figure things out with it. You know when it is working. And for the most part, you have complete control over it.

There is another very important part of your brain called your "Subconscious Mind." Your Subconscious is the part of your brain that takes in information and then (without any help from you), looks for ways to put that information to use. You will not be aware of your Subconscious, but know that it is recording everything. It is like a Court Reporter. It records every single thing (all of the things that are in your Conscious Mind and all of the things that aren't). A lot of information will come into your brain and you won't even be aware of it. You may be concentrating or have all of your attention focused on something else, so your Subconscious, like a reporter, picks up all of the details. It doesn't judge information to tell whether it is true or not, its function is to make sure that it is all recorded.

When it gets information that is the same, over and over again, or if your Conscious Mind says "This is important, I better remember this," your serious Subconscious will make a CD recording of it for you. And because your brain doesn't like for it to be completely quiet, your Subconscious just pops in a CD of something that it recorded earlier. It's like, when you go into a department store and they have soft music playing in the background. You don't even pay attention to it, but it is still playing. Your Subconscious gives you background music (or words) all the time.

You want to test your Subconscious? Think of a television show, commercial or video that you have seen many, many times. Think of the song or words that go along with it. Can you say them? You probably can (and you didn't even have to rehearse).

One of the parts of you that the Media really wants is your Subconscious Mind. They know that your Subconscious does not have a sense of humor AT ALL. It takes everything literally. If you keep hearing over and over again that some product, idea, service or lifestyle is important or good, your Subconscious will believe it, and make you a "CD-like" recording that you can play as your background music or words as you go through your day.

Remember, your Subconscious mind does not judge the information that comes into your precious vehicle. You are going to have to do it. After your Subconscious has made a CD for you, listen and make sure that the information is correct, healthy and good for you. Your mind is another one of your "sacred spaces", so you have to protect it. Sometimes the decisions you make to protect your valuable internal CD collection are not going to be popular. Know that everything is being recorded. In order to protect yourself from your Subconscious making tapes and CDs that are not good for you, you may have to change the channel or turn off the television set sometimes. When you watch it, make sure that **Intuition** is right there with you.

The same thing is true with songs, videos - everything that you see and hear. Your Subconscious Mind makes a recording for you to play over and over again inside your head. What you have recorded will affect how you act, what you wear, what you buy, and what you think and believe. Don't just let anything and everything play inside your vehicle.

What have YOU got recorded?

"I Want to Look Like the Girls in the Magazines"

TV, magazines and ads always show the "perfect" female body - flawless. The "perfect" hair, the "perfect" skin, the 'perfect' size, the "perfect" shape, and the "perfect" color. What is PERFECT? The word 'perfect' means: "complete, and exact, needing nothing." Life is constantly changing and moving. Yesterday my skin looked "perfect" and then I woke up today with a big zit on my chin. Perfection, whatever the standard, is hard to maintain in real life. Why? Because in order to maintain perfection, life has to stand still. Nothing can change. And if it's "perfect", why would you even want it to change? The reason magazine ads work is because we buy into the idea of perfection. We look at the girl in the ad and sometimes think "I want to look like her." "Her skin is perfect." I'll let you in on a little secret, "the girls in the magazines rarely look exactly like they do in the magazines." Computers are amazing and you can do all kinds of incredible things with them.

Why do they show "perfect" images of people in magazines and advertisements? To get you to feel not so perfect. If you feel complete and whole without their product or service, then they wouldn't make any money. Think about it.

Aspire to be the "perfect" YOU…always changing, growing and getting better from the inside out. Show the world the best YOU every day!

Magazines Don't Always Show You the Truth

For example:

Me   plus

this ⟶
(a small toy about the size of your hand)

became…

Wow! (but it's not reality)

So, Don't Believe The Hype!

The majority of the pictures that you see in magazines have been altered, airbrushed or changed in some way...

Now, unless you have someone who's going to walk around with you to airbrush your "imperfections," then that's a different story...

Yeah, ok, I got caught up…

Just remember – it's not real!
(In fact, if you think this is cool,
you might want to consider becoming a
Graphic Designer or a Photo Retoucher).

"Nothing great is created suddenly, any more than a bunch of grapes or a fig".
— Epictetus

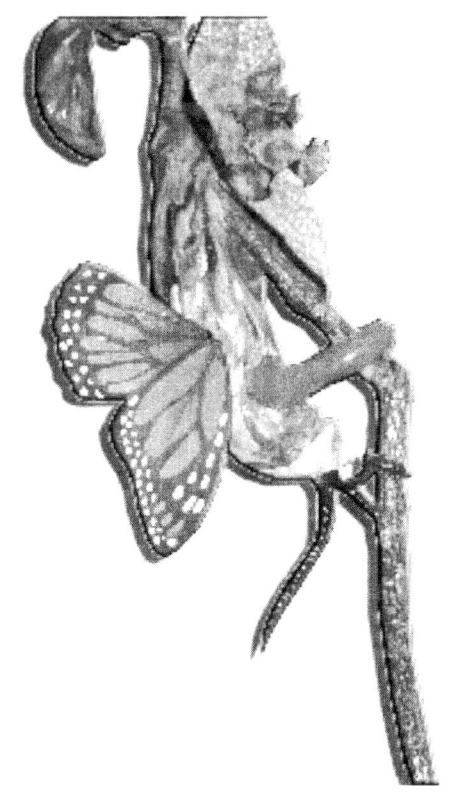

Phase Three: The Cocoon
Being With Myself

— *Chapter 11* —

"Why is it Always About SEX?"

What's Love Got to Do With It?

Everything and Nothing. Sometimes love can be attached to sex and sometimes it isn't. One thing you need to know is that there really is no such thing as "casual" or "no-cost" sex. Because you are not just a physical being, every time you allow someone into the sacred space of your body, they are also attaching themselves to not only your body, but your mind and spirit as well. Sex is never just physical. The physical act of sex may occur between two people who are not in love, or even care about or like each other, but when they have sex it creates an invisible connection between the two of them. You are a spiritual being. Any time you have sex with someone, it creates an invisible cord (or bond) between you and that person. As a female you will feel the effects of sex in three main areas:

- **Your body**

You may become pregnant. Also, any time you have unprotected sex and do not know the complete sexual and drug history of the person you are sleeping with (male or female), you are putting yourself at risk of contracting AIDS and other sexually transmitted diseases.

- **Your Mind**

It will affect how you feel about yourself - positively or negatively.

- **Your Spirit**

It creates spiritual cords to your sexual partner.

Just because you can't see the cords with your physical eyes, doesn't mean that the cords aren't there.

Part of your Girl Power is the fact that you are a receiver. Your body contains the seeds of life - you are like Mother Earth. You have the natural ability to cultivate life and love. There is a light and energy that radiates from you just because you were born a girl child. Your energy is powerful (don't ever under estimate it.) Girl Power is REAL. When you really begin to understand how wonderfully awesome you are, you will change the world! Men and boys have different natural abilities and gifts (they are wired differently - not "better" or "worse" - just different). Because of the way you are designed, and the awesome responsibility that you have in being a girl, your "love" choices are very important.

Why is sex illegal for children? Because sex is not just sex. It is an emotional, physical and spiritual connection. Anytime someone enters your body, they leave a part of themselves with you. And because of the spiritual and physical connection, every time you sleep with someone, you are also sleeping with everybody that they have slept with. That is a lot of energy that is being deposited into your body.

When you are young, you lack experience. Your love and understanding of yourself and others is still developing. It would be like picking a piece of fruit off of a tree before the fruit has ripened and had a chance to fully develop. When an adult has sex with ANY person who is not an adult, it is sexual abuse. It is not about love, but about taking or using your Girl Power. It is like moving into a new house and before you have had an opportunity to check out all the rooms, someone breaks in and steals treasures you didn't even know you had. You will never be the same. How can you "just get over it?" especially since you can't move out. You may find yourself hiding all the evidence so that you can go on with life and look normal to others. (If someone has broken in or is violating your sacred space, pleasE let an adult that you feel safe with know. If that doesn't work, listen to your Intuition and find another person - keep talking until somebody hears you and does something about it.)

One of the reasons that sexual abuse is hard to get over is because of the spiritual cords. Each time you engage in sex with the same person, the cord gets thicker and thicker. When you have been sexually molested, you don't want to be attached to the person that has harmed you - but you are. Your body will never be the same. It affects the relationship you have with your body and yourself, and the relationships that you have with other people.

The good news is that you CAN break and disconnect unwanted sexual cords. Each person is different and the amount and strength of the cords differ. Healing is always possible. It may take a lifetime to unravel many of the strings and cords that are attached to you. Be patient and loving with yourself. Don't take responsibility for bad decisions that the adults around you have made.

"What's love got to do with it?" Everything. It is going to require you to develop a deep love and compassion for yourself (especially when you feel sad, depressed and angry).

Love is going to require that you not just throw your body (your mobile home) away just because someone may have broken in and violated you.

You can always rehab - rebuilding from the inside out. Room by room. It's not going to be easy, that's why growing in love for yourself is so vital, because you are definitely worth it.

When something (or someone) is harmful to you - don't keep it secret. When you don't keep secrets, you become empowered - NO ONE (not even you) can hold anything over you.

That's REAL Girl Power!

Releasing Previous Sexual Encounters
(Cutting the Cords)

Go back and re-read Chapter 4, "Creating Sacred Spaces." (Again, find a place that is quiet and safe.) Close your eyes and think about your body. Breathe slowly and deeply. Using your Third Eye, see the inside of your body. Starting at the top of your head, check and see how every part of your body feels. Do this all the way down to your feet. If you find parts of you that are tense, tell yourself that you are safe, breathe deep and slow, and begin to relax that part of your body.

After you are completely relaxed, continue to close your eyes and see your heart. Visualize that you have cords attached to your heart that connect you to the people you have had sexual relations with. Each person has a different cord. Look for the cords that represent each person that you want to release.

Think about your energy. Feel your heart energy. Visualize all of your energy gathering around your heart area. As your heart grows in energy and heat, see your heart being filled with a red and gold light. For each of the cords send your energy like a bolt of lightening to the cord that you want to disconnect from you. See the cord melt away. You may only be able to break one cord at a time. If your heart feels sad or broken after you disconnect a cord, fill that empty space where the cord was with green and pink light.

Then go up to your head, and with your Third Eye, see if you can sense any cords there (mental ropes). Visualize the bolt of energy light and melt the cords. Fill the empty space where the cords were with a bright white and blue light.

After you are done, completely relax your body again. Continue to breathe slowly and deeply. When you are ready, open your eyes.

Now would be a good time to write your thoughts and this experience in your journal. Allow yourself to release any tears that may want to leave your body. Give yourself a great big "pink" hug.

(This exercise can be done over a period of time. You may be able to only melt one cord at a time. Some cords may be resistant and it may take several different times to completely melt them away. That is why it is so important to slow yourself down sometimes and check-in with yourself.

Don't forget to listen to your friend and companion "Intuition."

One last thing, this exercise does not take the place of talking with a professional therapist or counselor. (Sometimes we need all the support we can get.)

**THIS DOES NOT MEAN
THAT YOU SHOULD GO OUT AND HAVE SEX
SO YOU CAN DISCONNECT THE CORDS.**

**THIS IS NOT A GAME.
TAKE YOURSELF SERIOUSLY.**

The fact that you have the ability to love deeply - is one of the reasons that you want to handle your heart with care. Protecting your heart will be like walking a tightrope - it won't always be the easiest thing to do. Loving someone else more than you love yourself will make you lose your balance. So it's very important that you save a good portion of your "heart love" for you. You will need to show love and compassion to yourself for the rest of your life.

Your heart is a strange thing - the way it works is, the more you love YOU, your heart grows and you will have more love to give to others.

Loving you means:

- **not saying** mean and hurtful things inside your head or out loud <u>about</u> and <u>to</u> you.

- **making good** and healthy choices for your body, mind and spirit.

- **slowing down** so you can get to know yourself better.

- **listening** to "Intuition"

- **treasuring** your sacred space by not inviting just ANYBODY in (into your body or your life)

- **cultivating** your gifts and talents

- **developing** your character

- **nurturing** and being gentle with you

You don't have to lock your heart up and not love in order to protect it. But you do have to take care of your heart, because through loving you - you teach others how to love you too.

Looking for "Daddy Love" in All the Wrong Faces & Places

One of the most important relationships you will ever have - is the relationship with your parents. There are certain things that every child needs from both their mother and their father in order to grow up healthy (physically, mentally, emotionally and spiritually.)

Some of the things that a child needs from <u>both</u> parents are:
- unconditional love
- emotional and physical availability and support
- clean clothes
- safety (a safe place to live, and safe people around them)
- words of encouragement and support
- hugs, kisses and smiles
- to be taught what is good and bad behavior
- financial support
- to be taught that it is ok to make mistakes sometimes
- guidance (in developing decision making, problem solving, and conflict resolution skills)
- a spiritual foundation (which includes meaningful moral standards, values and a belief system)
- nutritious meals daily
- care when they are sick

- emotional stability
- time spent laughing and playing with them
- help in learning boundaries with themselves and others
- help in creating a positive self identity
- to "feel" special, and accepted

All the things listed are what every child needs in order to grow up healthy, balanced and self-confident.

We need both our mothers and our fathers in order to fully understand who we are. The relationship that we have with them will affect us all of our lives. Why?

I would imagine that if we could see what our "feeling" or "emotional" heart looks like - it would look something like this.

The Creator reserved a special place in your heart for both your mother and your father. The relationship that we have with our parents teaches us so many things. When they love and support us, we learn how to love and support ourselves. We learn who we are through our relationship with them, and through their relationship with each other.

Being a parent is a very important responsibility. It takes both a mother's and a father's love to complete a child's "emotional" heart.

Some children (through no fault of their own), do not grow up with their birth parents. There are many different reasons why this can happen.
- one or both parents are too young to take care of the child
- the birth parent(s) dies
- the parents divorce or are no longer in a relationship with each other
- a parent creates a child with someone that they did not want to create a child with
- the parent(s) were unsafe for the child to stay with (using too much alcohol and/or drugs or physical abuse)

- the parent(s) neglected or abandoned the child
- the parent(s) decided to create a child for someone else to parent
- the parent(s) may be in jail or prison

Can you think of any other reasons why a child might not grow up with their birth parent(s)? Write them in your workbook or journal.

When the birth father is missing from a child's life and there is no other father available to fill all of the child's needs, it leaves a "Daddy Love" empty space in the child's heart. Even if the mother remarries or is in a relationship with someone who lives with her and the child, if that person doesn't give the child all of the things that a child needs from a Daddy, then the "Daddy Love" hole is still there.

Even if the birth daddy is available, if all of the child's needs are not met (look back at the list), then a hole remains - it just may not be as big.

The same thing happens when the birth mother is not there. The "Momma Love" hole stays empty if there is no other "Mother Love" to replace it. Even if the birth mother is there, if she is not able to meet all of the child's needs - then a momma hole remains.

Whether they are good, bad, caring, nice, mean, emotionally or physically abusive or distant, the relationship you have with your parents will affect the relationship that you have with yourself. Our parents help to validate who we are in the world.

We need love and affection. We need "Daddy Love" and "Momma Love." When our birth parents are unavailable to fill our love heart, we may try to fill it through other people. Many times we try to fill the "Daddy Love" portion of our heart through the men we choose to be in a relationship with. Sometimes the 'Daddy Love' need is so big. It is like walking around on an empty stomach. When you are physically hungry, and can't have a good nutritious meal, if you get hungry enough, you may find yourself eating anything that is available (even if it is not good for you). Sometimes, love emptiness can cause us to settle for any attention.

We may think that even negative attention is better than no attention because it helps us to fill the space. But that is not true. If you are hungry for love and affection, it is easy to mistake sex for love. For example, if when you were a little girl, your father was not available (he may have died, was incarcerated, had problems with drugs and alcohol addiction, was physically distant, unloving, abusive or just not there), some of the life challenges that you may have to get through could deal with learning lessons around abandonment, boundaries and trust.

You may have gotten the idea when you were just a little girl (based on what you saw and lived through) that the world was a very unsafe and disappointing place. Also, that not only was the world an unsafe place, but more specifically, men were unsafe. You may have also gotten the idea that you are not valuable because you weren't born into a more healthy and complete environment. (And that is DEFINITELY not true.)

Because you are a spiritual being, your spirit knows the truth about why you may have been born into your situation - and the lessons you are to learn. The lessons may be completely different than what you think (they usually always are).

Your little girl spirit (most people call her your Inner Child) knows that you are worth more than you believe you are. Your Inner Child will continue to seek out men who she believes is like your birth dad. Your Inner Child may feel that if you choose someone with the same qualities as your dad, this time she will be able to "fix it" and get all of the things that she needed. So she will help you choose boys and men that will recreate your childhood experience in some way.

Daddies teach us who we are, what our value is as girls, and how to be treated by other males. We learn the importance of men in our lives and how to set boundaries and bond with them.

Mommas teach us who we are, what our value is as girls, the importance of self-care and boundaries. They also teach us the role men play in our lives and how they should treat us.

Your "little girl" spirit views things as if she were writing and directing a play with you as the main character. Join me for a behind-the-scenes look at:

"Family Life Theatre"

I've saved you a front row seat...

<u>Setting the Stage</u>

Sometimes you may wonder, "Why do I act the same way as my mother? My mother always chooses men that cheat on her, drink too much and beat her. Now that I am dating, I find that I am attracted to the same kind of man."

If this sounds familiar or like someone you may know, let me tell you a little story...

This story has many characters but the most important one is the Inner Child - played by Kesi (whose African name means: *"born when her father had difficulties"*).

When she was a child, Kesi decided that she would write a play about her family and then, one day star in it. She, of course, was in charge of the play because she took lots of good notes.

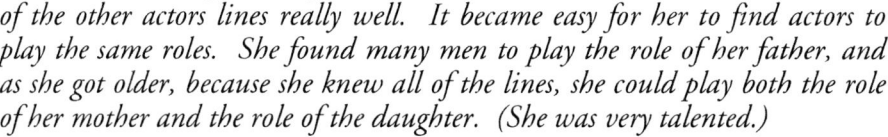

Even though Kesi didn't write the original script, she studied all of the characters - especially the role of the Momma, the Daddy and of course her part (the little girl).

When Kesi got older, she had memorized the original script and all of the other actors lines really well. It became easy for her to find actors to play the same roles. She found many men to play the role of her father, and as she got older, because she knew all of the lines, she could play both the role of her mother and the role of the daughter. (She was very talented.)

None of her real life relationships ever ended with "and they lived happily ever after." So, she continued to seek out new actors. But guess what? "Happily ever after" was yet to be found. She had chosen many actors to play the parts, but they kept doing the same things over and over again: treating her bad, abusing her, not being there emotionally for her, and she couldn't figure out why.

Kesi finally realized that she had to write a different script. She had to unlearn all of her old lines and learn new ones. Only then would she be able to rewrite the script for all of the other supporting actors. She was the star of the show. Kesi realized that it would not be easy to unlearn the part she had been playing for years, because she had volumes of videos, CDs and DVDs of the play. It was familiar. It was like the words to her favorite song. But in order for her play to have a different ending - she had to get some additional training and support. She had to figure out what was missing from the original script.

Uncovering and discovering the missing pieces in the script made Kesi mad, scared and sad. She was especially mad at her birth parents. Her unhappiness seemed to be their fault. She soon realized that the man and the woman who originally played her mom and dad (her birth parents) were just playing the roles that they learned as a kid - using the same lines that they saw and heard their parents use. Realizing that helped her to not be so mad at them, and eventually, she could possibly forgive them.

She had to some how rewrite the script so that her character would have all of the missing pieces. Changing the script was a lot of work. It took many days of rehearsals - being with herself, studying herself and being patient with herself in order for her to learn her new part.

The work was well worth it, because after she spent lots of time learning her new role - she found new actors to play the characters in a different way. She was sad, lonely and confused in the original script - now she is happy, balanced, secure and empowered. She is everything that she imagined herself to be, and more.

As the audience watches her performance, she can hear "BRAVO! Lessons learned!"

The End - or rather, The Beginning....

Just like Kesi, the same cast of characters may have been in your family for many generations. But with your magnificent Girl Power (and your Inner Child), you can create a whole new storyline for yourself. You can write a new script to hand down to your children.

Each time men (young and old) come into your life, when you feel yourself being attracted, slow down. Take some time to ask yourself, "Am I attracted to this man because I think he would be perfect to play a role in the "old" (original) script, or is he better suited for the "new" (and improved) script?" Better yet, ask Intuition - it will always tell you the truth.

One of the best ways to fill the empty "Momma and Daddy Love" spaces in your heart - is with love from the Creator.

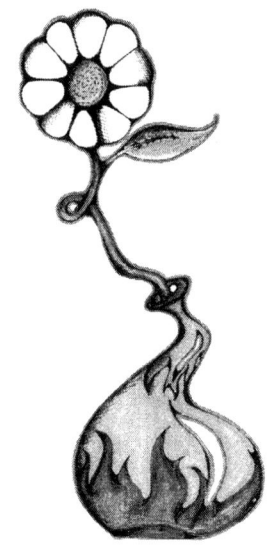

— *Chapter 12* —
Let's Talk About Boys...

"Boys. What's Up With Boys?"

Boys to men. Sometimes they can seem like some pretty strange creatures. There are definitely some major differences between males and females. Boys typically are raised differently then girls. Physically, biologically, mentally and emotionally, we are different, as well.

As much as they may frustrate us, make us angry, laugh, be confused, or cause us to cry, sing and dance, we need them and they need us. Even if you choose to never be in a romantic relationship with a boy or a man, in order for your life to be balanced and complete, you will have to have them in your life in some way (we all have daddies, brothers, play brothers or cousins). There is no way to get around it. The best thing we can do is to gain knowledge about ourselves, and then learn as much about them as we can.

As African-Americans, we have had a lot of things happen in the past that have added to our lack of understanding, confusion and mistrust of one another. Many girls and women will say, "All men are dogs," and many boys and men will say, "All women are bitches" (which are really female dogs). If the majority of both sexes think and feel that way, it really is no surprise that we don't get along. Why can't we trust each other?

Well, let's rewind the video tape for a real quick history lesson...

It all began when our ancestors were living in Africa. The continent of Africa is huge, in fact, you could fit the entire United States in it three times - that's how big it is. Because of its size, there are many different countries in Africa, each having their own customs, laws, languages and styles. The two things that they all had in common were that:

1). they honored their elders and ancestors and
2). all adolescents went through a rites of passage into manhood or womanhood

When our ancestors were kidnapped and forced into slavery, almost all of them were young boys and girls (teens and pre-teens.) Millions and millions of young people were enslaved because they were strong, healthy and could work for many, many years. So, many youth were forced to leave their families, friends and their communities. A lot of them were unable to even go through their rites of passage into adulthood. A big part of what a boy learns through his "rites of passage" is how to be a man as well as how to protect and provide for his family. That is important to remember, because not only were they traumatized by being kidnapped from their homes, they also were not completely trained or had the experience of adulthood.

Leaving Africa was indescribable. There were no "good byes.". Before they were placed in the bottom of the ships for the long journey to America or the Caribbean, the males and females were stripped of all clothing and personal belongings. They were tortured, beaten, shackled, chained, renamed, and then separated from each other. The males were always kept away from the females, probably because the slave traders knew that together they would be much stronger as a group. The journey was so horrible that it is known as the "Maafa" (the Middle Passage or Black Holocaust).

The trip was extremely long, stressful, and traumatic. Many became sick, died, were murdered, or committed suicide by jumping overboard. (Because you are here today, and you are reading this, is a testimony to their incredible strength and courage. If your ancestors had not survived, you would not even be here today. That is one of the reasons why we continue to remember, love and honor them)

When it finally became against the law to kidnap Africans and bring them to North America, slave owners began "breeding" slaves. (That means, because they needed more and more people to work the land, they made slaves have sex with each other in order to produce healthy offspring to work or to sell.) So African males (our great, great, great, grandfathers) were encouraged to have sex with as many females as they could to get them pregnant. The black male, who was able to father many children for slavery, was highly prized by the slave owner. Having very little else to feel proud of, black men became proud of their sexual ability.

Having a positive, healthy family relationship during slavery was out of the question and impossible to achieve. One or both could be sold away, or the slave master could decide that he wanted to have sex with the slave (male or female). Because they lacked the resources or options, any resistance could result in torture and/or death.

How did slavery affect black men and women? Both males and females were negatively affected. The African man (remember he came here as a young boy), didn't have the support of his original community. He had no resources (other than his sexual ability and strength). Many times, he knew of or witnessed an African young girl or woman being raped by the slave owner or other men. Because he was enslaved, he was unable to protect or provide for the woman. [Many times, (even today), when a woman is raped, some people blame the person that has been raped. Some think that rape is about sexual pleasure, but it is really a very violent crime.] Because the pain was so great (and no one was available to counsel our ancestors), many times the man would blame the woman (it is easy to blame others when we feel powerless ourselves).

The enslaved African woman, didn't have control over her body and her sacred spaces. Because the enslaved males could not protect her nor provide for her, she began to mistrust his strength and love for her. Many times, she would become pregnant by the slave owner. The child that was produced would be lighter in complexion and would have better treatment by the slave owner (remember, they were his children). She wanted her children to survive, so the lighter in complexion they were, the better the opportunity for them to survive. The black males would see how the black females would be more excited each time she had a lighter skinned child. Because they were unable to express their feelings, he didn't know that she was hurting just as much as he was, he grew to doubt himself and mistrust her even more. So when an enslaved woman was raped, and the enslaved man could not protect and provide for her, his anger toward himself, the slave owner and enslaved women grew even more.

Slave owners showed no respect for the enslaved woman, treating her as if she were not a real person. Because she was not valued for her incredible mind and intelligence, she began to believe that her body was her identity and worth. Over time, she learned to use her body to find favor with the slave owner.

Because their life was hard, they didn't have time to sit down and talk to each other about all of the many feelings and emotions they were experiencing. There were no psychologists to help them to process their feelings nor did they have the knowledge and wisdom of their native Africa. So our ancestors chose to deal with the pain in various ways. Some chose to emotionally detach (which means that they didn't allow themselves to get emotionally close to others). Some chose to act out violently toward each other instead of to the slave owner, because they would be killed. Some chose to misuse alcohol. And some chose all three.

The mental, emotional and spiritual trauma of slavery has never been effectively addressed by many African-Americans, and the emotional scars continue to be passed down from generation to generation. Even many years after the official end to slavery, it still is not easy being a black male or female in today's society. Today, black girls and woman are still thought of as sexual objects. You can see it in how we are portrayed in movies, videos and magazines. (Black boys and men are portrayed as "players" and as being irresponsible.) Because we continue to see these images and the memory of abuse that we carry from our ancestors, can you understand why we have feelings of anger and mistrust of one another?

There is a lot of healing work that has to happen between us in order for us to have healthy relationships with each other. Just as girls and women are "looking for daddy love in all the wrong places and faces," boys and men are "looking for daddy love too." African-American males don't have men in their lives that don't carry the scars of slavery. Very few have ever had an opportunity in this country to fully be empowered as men.

It all may seem pretty overwhelming. What can you do? First and foremost, recognize that your pain may run deeper than you think. Get to know yourself and examine your self image and the things you believe about black girls and women, and then the things you believe about black boys and men. Know that you cannot change anyone but yourself.

What can you change or improve? Change or improve the conversations you have in your head and out loud about YOU. Don't just talk to yourself any ole kind of way, because then you will allow others to talk that way to you, too.

Begin to critically look at how black girls and women are portrayed in the media and demand that changes be made. How? By not supporting things that don't support and respect you. Speak up and out. Show yourself some love.

If you want a boy to like you for more than just your body, you have to show him more than just your body. (If a boy really likes you, he wants you to say "No" because he wants to know that you aren't easy to sleep with.)

Don't "dress to impress" but rather, "dress to bless." Dress to be a blessing to yourself and others. We need to see positive images of young girls and women who are using more than just their bodies to gain love, money and success. We need to see more images of black girls and women showing themselves respect and gaining respect from black men. The world is watching what you do (don't underestimate your tremendous girl power).

And lastly, if you are one of the girls or women who believes "all men are dogs," go back to the previous chapter, re-read it, and see how you can rewrite your script to include brothers who are trying to do the right thing. (It is important for you to change your script, or you will not recognize them when they show up in your life.)

That's some of what's up with boys...

As boys are often referred to as "Dogs," are you feeding the dogs? Are they sniffing around outside your door? How do you carry yourself? Remember, gaining RESPECT is different than just gaining ATTENTION.
You are much more than the sum of your parts.

"I want to have Sex with you" can sound a lot like "I Love You" if you are not really listening.

"If you love me, you'll do it."
doesn't mean – *"I respect you and want the best for you."*

"Can I get your number?"
doesn't mean – *"I want a relationship."*

"I'll be careful."
doesn't mean – *"I really care what happens to you."*

"You feel so good."
doesn't mean – *"I want you to feel good about yourself."*

"You are my lover."
doesn't mean – *"You are my only lover."*

"I need you."
doesn't mean – *"I'll be there when you need me."*

"Don't you trust me?"
doesn't mean – *"You can trust me because I care about you."*

"You are so fine."
doesn't mean – *"I love you."*

Are you hearing what is really being said, or are you just hearing what you want to hear?

Being a Couple

Choosing to be in a relationship with someone is a very important decision to make. In African culture, it was not just the couple that was joining. When a young man decided to be in a relationship with a young woman, it was a joining of two communities (all of the people that were in his life - his family and friends, and all of the people that  were in her life - her family and friends). There were elders to help counsel the couple. It became not only the couple's responsibility to uphold the union, but the couple was accountable to the entire community.

**A relationship is a serious thing.
Future families and communities
can come out of relationships.**

In this society, we are taught to think about relationships in a different way. When two people decide to become a couple, rarely (if at all) do we get advice from our families and the people who love us. Many times we look at the outside of a person (how they look) and based JUST on that, we decide whether we want to be in a relationship with them.

It would be like going to a store to choose a very important gift. When you walk in, you see a lot of fancy, beautifully wrapped boxes. Instead of opening the boxes to see if the present inside is what you want, you choose the box that has the prettiest ribbon on the outside. The box could be completely empty, full of junk or contain a valuable and rare jewel. The jewel could be inside of a plain box. Worthless rocks could be inside the fancy, expensively wrapped box, but you wouldn't be able to tell just by looking at the outside of the boxes.

Unfortunately, that is how we sometimes choose the people we allow inside of our bodies and sacred spaces. How can you sometimes tell what is on the inside of your potential boyfriend's package? Before you commit to having him as a boyfriend, be his friend. Watch how he treats the women in his life, (his mother, his sisters, his last girlfriend). Does he respect women? (Don't go by what he SAYS but what he DOES.) Bring him around the people you care about and who care about you. If he doesn't want to meet the people that are important in your life, then he may not want to really be in your life. If the people you care about and who care about you don't like him, TAKE NOTICE! They may see things about him that you can't. Remember the African proverb:

"Don't be so much in love that you can't tell when the rain comes."

Wanting to have sex with you does not automatically mean that you are a "couple". You may think you are in a committed relationship, while he may be just having sex.

How can he pass up an opportunity to be with an incredibly talented, unique, beautiful, and loving person like you? Well, males and females really are wired differently.

Most girls and women are raised to believe that a woman is less valuable without a man to take care of her. Even when we are little girls, we are read fairy tales with the princess having to be rescued by the prince. They find true love and live "happily ever after." Unfortunately, most boys aren't looking for the "one girl" to live happily ever after with.

There are many reasons why your goals may be different. For one, males carry within their bodies billions of potentially fertile sperm. This, along with their hormones, can make a boy always want to have sex. The hormone testosterone creates a great deal of tension inside of his body (especially sexual tension). It makes him think about having sex much of the time. When, and if he can't have sex with someone, some males release the natural tension that builds up in their bodies on a daily basis through masturbation and/or, in another healthy way by participating in or watching sports. Some do it in unhealthy ways by being overly aggressive toward others (being abusive, picking fights, etc).

When a boy is a teen or in his early twenties, it is the time when his body is really flooded with testosterone, and it creates quite an imbalance for him. His body may be driving him to release sperm but his mind may not be completely clear on how to manage it. His goal is to have sex, and he may say just about anything to get it.

Just like your body is your vehicle and has many functions that are automatic, his body is his vehicle too. Boys' and men's bodies are designed to function this way, and that is the way it has worked since humans have been on the planet.

Another influence is the media. When you see movies and videos, if males have a lot of females around them, they are considered more desirable. Men know that other men are pretty much wired the same way, so to have lots of girls and women around, can mean to other women (and men) that he has it going on.

His goal is Quantity and he may not even be consciously aware of it. (Remember, he has billions of sperm that are anxious to be released.) Also, don't forget the messages that were passed down through the generations and how enslaved black males were valued for their ability to get many enslaved black females pregnant.

It's a natural, cultural, biological, physical, hormonal thing all mixed together.

As a young man matures emotionally, and learns about himself and his body, he is able to control his natural urges and balance out his need for sexual release and his natural need for love and companionship. But it takes time and maturity. (Don't be fooled into thinking that maturity is an "age thing." Maturity is based on the individual and the decisions they make. There are wise young people and foolish old people.) That is why it is so important to get to know a boy first. Become friends. Find out where his head is.

For most girls and women, our bodies motivate us in a different way. Eggs are more complex than sperm and take a larger investment of energy to produce. Every female is born with a limited amount of eggs that grow to maturity (approximately 300-500.) We don't constantly produce them like sperm. Having only 300-500 mature eggs to work with versus billions of sperm, young women would do better to go for

Quality instead of Quantity. Your body is designed for you to naturally be selective. If you look at other animals in nature, it is the same way.

I often used to wonder why in the animal kingdom, the male species was always more decorative and sometimes elaborate. (Look at the male peacock, and lion for example.) The Creator designed them to get the female's attention and to indicate that they are healthy, since even in nature, the female species has to be selective. Just like with animals, your offspring will have a better chance of survival if you choose a male that is going to stick around.

Boys and men depend on us being selective. Even if he tells you something different, he wants to know that your sacred spaces are truly sacred. I have heard many males say, "There are girls you have sex with, and then there are girls that you have relationships with." Even getting pregnant is not going to make a young man have more of an investment in you. If he doesn't really know you, love you, respect you and has AGREED that he wants to have children with you, he has already gotten to his goal. More than likely, he will move on. Some will stick around if you are having sex with him on a regular basis, but in the long run, he will probably choose to be with the girl that he is emotionally attached to rather than the one that he is just physically "kickin it" with.

Now, some girls will say that they don't care about being in a relationship. It's all about just having sex. Well, you should care. You are a spiritual being and your body is sacred. Misuse of sex can be an indication of an addiction just like drugs and alcohol. It can be a way of filling our "Daddy Love" need. If you allow everybody into your body - you lose value in the eyes of others. But most importantly, you lose value to yourself. It will definitely affect your self-esteem.

If the only way you think you can keep him is with your body, then you don't really have him.

Life is a journey, and you will meet all TYPES of people and have all kinds of meaningful relationships - all of them definitely shouldn't be about SEX. Boys and men are going to come into your life for many different reasons, and they are not always for the reasons we may think.

Sometimes people show up to:
- help us be stronger by testing us
- help us to see that we need to love ourselves more
- help us learn to set boundaries and say "No" when we need to
- support our life mission and goals

All boys that are cute and may be nice to us aren't supposed to be our boyfriends. Some are supposed to be our brothers and friends.

Don't just give your precious eggs and sacred space away. If a man or a boy buys you things and you both don't really love each other but have sex anyway, are you exchanging your sacred space to ride in his car, for money or gifts? How many "goods" does he have to buy you in order to pay for "your goods?" Are you easily bought? Count up the cost.

Is it really worth it?   Are you giving away more than you keep?

There are three main parts to a healthy relationship:
Intimacy, Passion, and Commitment

Intimacy - refers to the feelings of closeness and affection and fondness. This is usually what we feel around our family, friends and loved ones. Usually feelings of Love are expressed.

Passion - is what leads to romance. Its driving force is physical attraction, sexual arousal and desire. This is usually what we feel around someone we are physically attracted to. Just having passion usually indicates a relationship with feelings of Infatuation and/or Obsession.

Commitment - is the desire to maintain the relationship through dedication. It should start off slow and grow more over time. This is usually what we feel when we decide to get married. It should include Love, Intimacy and Passion.

On this journey called life, you can choose the people who you will love, but you can't choose the people who will love you back. You can't make a person love you - no matter what you do for them or give them.

> **Why did he say:**
> *"I can't live with you"*
> **and**
> **Why did she say:**
> *"I can't live without you"*
> **Because he went north and she went south**
>
>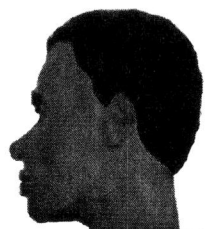
> **And they both lived.**
>

Ending a relationship that no longer serves your highest good - can feel like the end of the world. Take a deep breath and keep walking in the direction of the "New and Improved You." The You that makes good and healthy choices. The you that knows when and how to say "NO!" to things and people when it is the best thing to do.

What to Do When It's Time to Let Go

No matter what the circumstances, ending a relationship can be painful. It can be like trying to take apart two pieces of paper that were glued together. When you have a child or children with someone, and the relationship ends, it can sometimes be like trying to separate something that has been SUPER Glued together (it can be really painful).

- **Decide.** Is this what I really want?
- **Prepare.** Know that you may feel uncomfortable, sad, angry, scared, confused or depressed. Allow yourself to feel. Visualize the situation before you actually do it. See all of the possible responses. Practice what you will say and what you will do.
- **Choose.** Find a place that's private but is not secluded.

- **Communicate.** Explain why you feel this is best for you.
- **Mean it.** Stick to your decision. Remember what you practiced - and then put it into action.
- **Love.** Love yourself and give yourself time.

> *I can't pretend I love you when I don't.*
> *My mind can pretend, but my heart just won't.*
>
> *I can't be there and care, when I don't want to.*
> *So, what do I do when my mind says, "I love you?"*
>
> *I don't want to mislead you and*
> *guide you the wrong way -*
> *But when my heart doesn't beat for you,*
> *what am I supposed to say?*
>
> *I don't want to hurt you or make you cry*
> *because you are a friend.*
> *But, someday all the deception and lies*
> *have to come to an end.*
>
> *- Rachel McGaughy*
> *(age 18)*

When you are choosing someone to be in a relationship with, there is one very important thing that you should NEVER do. Don't ever choose someone without first consulting Intuition. Many girls and women ignore Intuition when it comes to boys and men, and many times regret it later.

Listen to your Intuition

Intuition knows that even if he looks good, but if he treats you bad, or you feel bad, then he's not the one for you.

— *Chapter 13* —
"*Finding My Posse*"

Choosing Friends

As you go through your life, choosing friends will be one of the most important decisions you will make. Friends play a critical role in our lives, because if we pay attention, the people we choose to have as friends, can tell us a lot about who we are. There is an old saying "Birds of a feather, flock together."

People sometimes choose people to be their friends because:
- they feel like they have a lot in common
- they admire something about the other person and want to be more like them
- they like the way they feel around that person (useful, smarter, prettier, happier, stronger, etc.)
- they know that they can trust the other person and feel safe around them

Who are your friends and why did you choose them?

When you look up at the moon, no matter where you are on the planet, you will not be able to see the front and the back of it at the same time. And just like the moon, if you look in a mirror, you will only be able to see one side of your self. To see the front and back of you at the same time, you will need another mirror.

We need our friends, because they can mirror the sides of us we can't see. They also help us to grow by seeing the parts of us that are hidden from our view. Choose your friends wisely.

Choose friends that can reflect and bring out the best parts of you.

The fact that life is always changing can be difficult, exciting and sometimes frustrating. People, places and things never stay the same. You may meet someone and think that you have found the perfect friend. They enjoy doing the same things you do, they laugh at all your jokes, make you feel really special, and they spend lots of time with you. And then one day (it happens so quickly that you don't even see it coming) - they change. They begin to do different things that you aren't really interested in, they start acting differently and begin hanging with other people besides you. It can be really hard when your friends change without warning you first.

**Don't hold on to People, Places and Things too tightly.
Learn to let them flow through your life bringing you gifts,
lessons and wonderful blessings.**

But just as you are on your journey to "butterflyhood," your friends may be too. Everybody is traveling (hopefully) fulfilling their life mission and purpose. Sometimes it can be a lonely journey. Remember, everybody's curriculum is different. It may not always be easy to stay connected with old friends when you grow (mentally, emotionally and spiritually), change schools, jobs, cities or states. There will be times when you have to let friends go in order to continue to grow.

You will meet people along your journey that will be in your life for your entire life, and some will only stay long enough to bring you gifts or support during some of your most challenging life lessons.

The beautiful gift in true friendship is that even though circumstances may change, the love and respect you have for each other can still remain. True friendship is always available - you may have to work at it though. Sometimes you will meet friends as caterpillars, and then, many years later reunite as butterflies.

Are you one of those people that you can count on as a friend?

Gossip

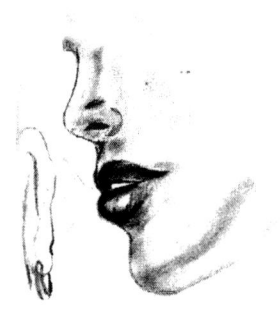

Gossip. It can be one of the most destructive habits we have. When you talk about someone else, it freezes the person, incident or people involved in time. It is not really fair, because life doesn't stand still. It doesn't give the person (or people) an opportunity to set the record straight or to apologize. Most of the time, the information that is being passed along is not completely accurate, and it is usually done to shame, embarrass or to hurt the people involved. If most people who gossip were to be honest about it, most gossip is spoken out of jealousy, envy or just plain meanness.

One good way to measure how bad you feel about yourself is to see how good you feel when you tell someone something bad about someone else. We are all here to learn lessons. Negatively commenting to others about someone (just for the sake of talking about them) is like a person coming in during the middle of a movie and wanting to tell everyone what the movie is about.

Don't cause others to fall because you're trippin'.

Many people don't understand a very simple universal law - it is the law of karma or reaping what you sow. When you send curses instead of blessings out - it is like a boomerang - it will definitely come back to you and at you. What you say about other people will be said about you, and what you wish for others you are wishing for yourself, too.

Your words are powerful.
Use your words to speak life and not death.

> *"If we could read the secret history of our enemies, we could find in each person's life, sorrow & suffering enough to disarm all hostility."*
>
> Author Unknown

Drugs & Alcohol

Drugs and alcohol. More than ever, you are being bombarded by advertisers, movies, videos and songs to drink, smoke and do drugs. The companies that make, sell and promote cigarettes and liquor, create advertisements that are specifically targeted to you. Why? Because they know that if they can convince you that buying their product will some how make you feel better, be more popular, sexy, and fun to be around, you will be a customer for life. They are investing in your future in a very negative way.

Alcohol and drugs are addictive. They don't really make you feel better, because whatever it was that you felt bad about before you started drinking, will still be there after you stop drinking. The more you stay medicated, drugged up, drunk, high, buzzed, and floating, the more passive you become. The moment you become hooked and you believe that this is the way to go, you begin to pay the price on your health, relationships. finances, spirit, and mental capabilities.

Not using drugs can be very challenging. It's hard to say "Don't do drugs," because we live in a society that believes in medicating problems. For every ache and pain that happens inside our bodies, there is a pill or a product that you can go to any drugstore and buy without having to see a doctor first.

Many people walk around with a lot of stored up disappointment and anger - which can lead to stress and pain in the body. (Remember, our bodies are designed to alert us when something is wrong so that we can fix it.) Instead of dealing with the issue that is causing the pain (why your internal alarm system is going off), it is easy to just take something that will make us temporarily feel better.

Say, for instance, your house alarm went off in the middle of the night. Instead of calling the police and making sure that you are safe, you put in some ear plugs, roll over and go back to sleep. That is how many of us have been taught to deal with pain.

You have the opportunity to do something different. When you feel scared, stressed, angry, or not confident, before you decide to medicate, ask yourself what is REALLY causing the pain. Don't just be satisfied with the answer "I just feel bad." Figure out why.

If you believe that Drugs are the Answer to your problems, What exactly is the Question?

Nothing is neutral. Everything you do either brings you closer to or further away from your life's mission and goals.

Why would you want to waste your time being WASTED?

●●●●●●●●●●●●●● *How Do You Party?*

Using drugs (especially alcohol) is seen in this society, as sort of a rites of passage into adulthood. The law says you can't purchase or consume alcohol or cigarettes until you turn 21. For some people, it is customary to go out on their 21st birthday and get drunk. Sometimes, when a person wants to feel more grown up, drinking can seem like a way to do it.

I remember (back in the stone ages) when I was a college student at a predominantly white school. I noticed there were some distinct differences in the way the majority of the white students "partied" and the way the majority of the black students "partied." For most white students, "partying" meant getting a keg of beer, or drinks, getting drunk and using drugs. There would be some dancing, but the main focus was on drinking. They even had contests to see who could drink the most.

"Partying" for me and most of the other black students, meant dancing 'til you were soaking wet with sweat. There may have been some alcohol and/or drugs available, but the main focus was on dancing, and we had a ball! The only side effects our partying caused were: underarm sweat stains in our clothes, sweated out hair, and sometimes sore feet.

The few times I "partied" with alcohol, didn't create a lot of fun to me. I didn't feel good the next day, my skin looked bad, I had a terrible taste in my mouth, and a headache. I decided that for me, "partying" was a lot more fun without drugs or alcohol.

Today, there seems to be more of a mixture of the two styles of "partying" - drinking and dancing. More artists are making songs and videos that encourage you to do the same. ("Pass the Courvoisier") The real down side of that, (especially for a female) is that alcohol and drugs will affect you differently than a male. How?

- Because women have less water in their bodies than men, drinking the same amount of alcohol as a man will get you more intoxicated. The alcohol is less diluted in your system and will have a greater impact.

- It will absorb a lot of the water in your body system, drying out your hair and skin.

- Heavy and or continued use can cause fertility problems.

- You are especially vulnerable to and at risk for sexual assault, date rape, unprotected sex, unwanted pregnancies and sexually transmitted diseases, including HIV/AIDS.

- If you drink while you are pregnant, your baby may be born with fetal alcohol syndrome (FAS), which is one of the leading known causes of mental retardation.

What does "partying" mean to you?

One of the reasons drugs are harmful is that drugs put your Intuition right to sleep. It can't help you. You are likely to be in dangerous situations and not realize it until it is too late. You become more risky in your behavior. All too often, sex and drugs go together. With Intuition asleep, overindulging in one, can set you up for the other. Things you normally wouldn't do become a lot easier to do, and can lead to unprotected sexual encounters. Which can lead to AIDS, which could kill you.

Just as you are a spiritual being, drugs and alcohol have "spirits," too. Drugs and alcohol are spirits that are looking for someplace to live, and if you welcome them in, they can take over your mind, body and spirit.

Black folks can be really susceptible to misusing drugs and alcohol. Many times, if nothing else is available, you can always make the choice to get high In many black neighborhoods, the temptation can be even greater, because liquor stores are everywhere. Somebody you know will probably have access to some (either at school, at home or in the neighborhood.) Many families have at least one person in it who has a drug or alcohol addiction problem. If drug or alcohol abuse runs in your family, don't think that you can't become addicted. If you are a consistent user of drugs and/or alcohol, admit it. Recognize that you may have a potentially serious problem, and seek help.

Your life is precious, and you came here on a special mission. Have an action plan. Don't allow yourself to repeat negative behaviors over and over again (generation after generation).

Some mistakes you can't even afford to make once.

Loving and Accepting Myself

(This should be done in front of a mirror.) Close your eyes and take at least 10 slow, deep breaths. With your Third Eye, think back to your earliest memories. How old were you? For the next five minutes, think of as many things as you can that you haven't asked yourself forgiveness for.

Open your eyes. Begin with the statement, "I forgive myself for..." Continue to repeat the words, "I forgive myself for..." until you feel complete. Make sure each time you say the statement, you are looking yourself in the eyes.

Now, close your eyes and take another 10 slow, deep breaths. With your Third Eye, once again think back to your earliest memories. For the next five minutes, think of as many things about you as you can, that you haven't expressed love for.

Open your eyes. Begin with the statement, "I love myself for..." Continue to repeat the words, "I love myself for..." until you have said the statement at least the same amount of times as you forgave yourself.

Repeat this exercise any time you feel disappointed or angry with yourself.

The more you forgive yourself - the more love you will have for yourself. The more love you have for yourself - the more you will be able to forgive yourself.

The best mind altering drug is
The Truth.

Peer Pressure

*"When you don't know who you are,
you're bound to act like anybody."*

Everybody wants to fit in. Sometimes, you may be tempted to not be as strong and confident as you can be because you may want others to like and accept you. Being accepted by our peers and feeling like we belong somewhere is very important. However, friendships that encourage you to engage in risky behaviors that may threaten your health or safety (perhaps because they may involve using drugs, engaging in unsafe sex, committing an act of violence or other crimes), can be a serious problem. It can alter the entire course of your life. One way to tell if there is a potentially serious problem with a friendship, is to look at how your behavior changes when you are around certain people, and when you are not. People come into our lives to teach us things about ourselves, about the other person or something else we should know. Sometimes it is to practice and/or find out what we really believe in and stand for.

The only time to show courage is when you're scared.

Resisting peer pressure can be pretty complex. Every day, you will be tested to see if you are emotionally strong enough to risk possible rejection by your peers or friends. Some days you may need to "lead" the group (because you have the best plans). Other days you may decide to "follow" (because someone else may have the better idea). Then there will be times when you may have to walk away alone because in your gut you know it is the right thing to do. You are going to have to decide.

There are consequences to every choice you make in life. Choose things that are going to serve your mission.

"Never spend time with people who don't respect you."
Maori Proverb

The important thing is to get in where you truly fit and not where others think you should be.

Who do you act like when you are with your friends?

Are you really being you?

Do you hide your light in order to fit in?

(If you have to hide your light - are they really your friends?)

One of the greatest gifts you can give to yourself is your own friendship.

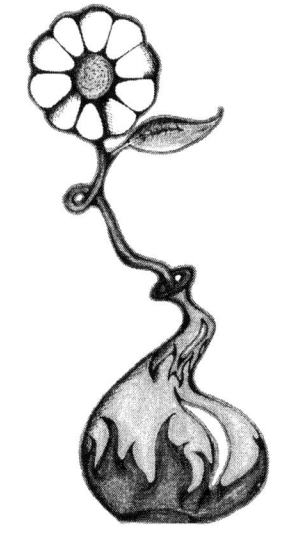

— *Chapter 14* —

"Why Do We Have to Die?"

"I Just Lost Someone I Really Care About."

"People don't truly die unless we stop remembering them"

Death. It is a subject that few people in this society feel really comfortable talking about. In this culture, we have been taught to view life as if it existed in a straight line: you are born, you grow in age, and then you die - the end.

In traditional African culture, death was seen as a circle and a necessary and important part of life. A person's life didn't end at death but merely changed forms. The spirit world was just as important as the physical world. Death was not seen so much as a tragedy but a transition - a type of graduation. Remember, everybody comes to earth with a purpose and a life mission. There are no accidents or mistakes, so when someone died, it was thought that they completed their physical life mission and returned home to the spirit world.

One reason people have to "transition" is to make room for new people on the planet. If no one ever died, what do you think would happen to the planet? Every human being has a round trip ticket to earth - not a "one way." Unfortunately, no one books their own reservations so it is impossible to determine when or how a person will leave. Life exists for however long it is supposed to exist. Things happen for reasons all the time. We are just not always aware of them.

**The Butterfly reminds us in whispers that life is a cycle.
It never ends - it just changes from one form to another.
(Some forms appear to be more beautiful than others.)**

Life and death can be like going with your family to Disney World. If you have ever been to Orlando, Florida, you know that in the hotel rooms, there is a Disney channel that shows you videos of what is happening at the amusement parks. You can actually sit in your hotel room all day just watching the television. What if your family went on a vacation to Disney World and instead of really getting out in the sunshine and riding the rides, you sat in front of the tv and watched other people enjoying themselves? What if you and your family stayed in the hotel the entire time and just watched the Disney vacation channel for an entire month? Then, before you knew it, it was time to go back home. All you got to do was WATCH other people have a good time. Well, you would probably be pretty upset (I know I would. I would be kicking, screaming and throwing a good ole fashioned two-year-old's tantrum.) You definitely would be upset about leaving. You were there for a whole month and never got a chance to participate! But what if your family went to Disney World, and you only saw your hotel room when you checked in, and then late each night when you came back to your room - exhausted from riding all the rides, sightseeing, eating, shopping and having a good time? What if you only stayed in your hotel room long enough to sleep, shower and change clothes - then got out the door again for another daily adventure? You got to see and do everything that Disney World offered! What if you did that for an entire month? When it was time to go home, you would probably be ready. You wouldn't protest, but would be ready to get back home to see loved ones and to tell them all about your amazing trip to Disney World!

Well, life and death can sometimes be like that. If you were to spend the majority of your life not doing what you came to "This World" to do. If you spent a good part of your life watching television (especially soap operas, sitcoms and movies) watching people act and pretend to have exciting lives, how would you be any different than someone who spent their entire vacation watching the Disney vacation channel? You are only here in "This World" for a short time. Everybody's stay is different. Just like in a hotel, everybody doesn't check in and out at the same time. And everybody doesn't go back home at the same time either.

Live your life in a way that when it ends (no matter how young or old you are), you have fulfilled your life's mission and purpose. Live each day as if it were your FIRST day of vacation. And when it is time to make your transition, hopefully it will be a joyous time - a celebration of a life fully lived and not just a time of grief and sorrow because you felt it was cut short.

Being in a physical body (using only a small portion of brain space) sometimes makes it hard to fully comprehend and understand the whole concept of death and transition. Frankly, one of the hardest parts is that death usually comes as a surprise (so you are never fully prepared when people that you love die). When our family and loved ones leave this earth to go back home to the spirit world, it is sometimes one of the most painful experiences of being a human being.

I remember when my oldest brother Ronnie (who was 32 years old at the time) was killed back in 1987 - his death really impacted me. He was seven years older than me, and his transition was the first time that I had ever had to experience the loss of an immediate family member. His murder was a shock to my entire family. Each of my family members experienced his transition in a different way. We experienced it differently because we each experienced HIM in a different way. We all had different relationships with him. For me, he was my big brother. I didn't fear him while he was physical, so I don't fear him in the spirit world. I talk to him and keep pictures of him around. I acknowledge his birthday as well as the day he made his transition. Many times (especially when I am going through something that only a "big brother" would understand), I talk to him out loud or in my mind. On many occasions when I have needed his help, he would show up in my dreams and I would have conversations with him.

My brother Ronnie was very protective and military-like. When I need extra protection or help, sometimes I will ask him to come and assist me or to send me the help that I need. I have never felt that he has not heard me. Our relationship is different than when he was alive, but still very real.

Religious activities, and spiritual beliefs keep you connected to your loved ones who have made their transitions, so explore your own beliefs.

I must admit, I don't fully understand all of the ins and outs and whys of life and death, but I do know that I don't fear it like I used to (life or death). Our African ancestors understood it. They understood that life was circular, and that energy cannot be destroyed, only changed.

Look at all of the different things you can do with water. Water can become liquid, steam, and solid (ice). In all of its forms, it's still water.

Value your life and be thankful for every day that you can breathe and see your loved ones. But also know that death is a very real part of life. Each day we wake up to a new day. Yesterday had to die to make room for today. Mother earth goes through a death in the winter to bring new life in the spring. Caterpillars die to make butterflies. Change comes in many ways. Sometimes you will not always understand it, but you have to trust that the Creator loves you, and that everyone's life is happening exactly the way it should.

I'm not afraid of death, it's the dying part that kills me.

Ways to Remember Loved Ones Who Have Made Their Transitions

There is an African proverb that says "No one ever truly dies until there is no one left who remembers them." If you have friends and loved ones that have made their transitions - continue to remember them by:

• Displaying photos of our loved ones that have made their transitions helps us to keep their memory alive and can stimulate conversations, funny and interesting stories associated with the person and an overall feeling of continued connection.

• Create a Living Memorial with pictures and mementos honoring their lives.

• Celebrate their birthday and Acknowledge the day they made their transition by doing something special on those days.

• Light a white candle and say a special prayer. Take a moment to remember those who have had meaning in your life.

Don't be discouraged by good-byes. A good-bye is necessary before you can meet again. And meeting again after moments or lifetimes is certain for those who are our loved ones and friends.

— *Chapter 15* —

"*Help! I Need Some Support Over Here!*"

"Who Are Ancestors?"

None of us stands alone, but we stand as a continuation of a long line of others. Our ancestors are all of the people who have lived before us that we are connected to. They are the people who have completed their mission on earth and have gone ahead to the spirit world.

Honoring ancestors is something that people from every culture have done since the beginning of time.

In this society we honor our collective ancestors on a daily basis. How? Through the images on our currency, and the names of holidays and other celebrations. Streets, cities, buildings, libraries and schools are named for famous ancestors. In Africa and other parts of the world, honoring personal ancestors are just as important. They are our family members who have gone on ahead and who assist us in the spirit world. As Africans in America, we have many ancestors that we share as a group: Dr. Martin Luther King Jr., Harriet Tubman, Nat Turner, Madame C.J. Walker, Malcolm X and others. We also have ancestors from our individual families: our great, great grandmothers and fathers, our great aunts and uncles and other family members who have made their transitions into the spirit world.

Honoring our ancestors reminds us that we are the present representatives of the accumulated lives of many generations that were before us. When we are born, we are connected to our mother through the umbilical cord. Even after the cord is cut, our connections with the past are never severed. Our parents give birth to us, just as their parents gave birth to them. We continue to stay connected. One way to honor them is to live your life in such a way that they would be proud to be your ancestor.

Our ancestors are waiting for us to learn from their mistakes, borrow from their courage and strength, and practice their wisdom.

What is a good measure of your success? It will be what your great, great grandchildren say about you.

What Are Rituals, and Why Are They Important?

Rituals are the way you do the things you do. Everyone has rituals that they perform on a daily basis. Look around you. It may be your daily ritual to get up at a certain time each day, go to the bathroom, brush your teeth and turn on the tv or radio to the same station every morning. It is your morning ritual. We all have physical rituals that we perform, but we should also have spiritual rituals as well. You are a Spiritual Being. Participating in a religion reminds you of that. What is "Religion" anyway? The word  "religion" comes from the latin word ligarei which means "to join or link." So the word religion means "to re-link humans and the divine." Religion should help you to remember your relationship with the Creator. Most times, we are born into our religion through our parents and their religious choices. They are the first to teach us about our spirituality. All across the globe, all cultures are set up the same way. Most people are Baptist, Catholic, Muslim or Buddhist for example, because that is what they were born into.

Sometimes, if your parents don't have a religion, it's easy for the children to not have one, too. Religion reminds you to develop a spiritual connection. Through participating in a religion, you learn about the Creator, how to pray and the rules and laws that help you develop your character. Although going to church every Sunday can make you religious, it doesn't necessarily mean that you are growing in your spirit. It is just like if you were to go to school. There are many things you can memorize in school, but they really only become important when you put them into practice in the real world.

The key is to decide what religion is best suited for you, and then make it your goal to develop a very real and personal relationship with the

Creator. Grow your spirit. The more you grow your spirit, the clearer your life mission and purpose will become.

Religion = the rituals that 're-link' you to the Creator

Spirituality = what you do with that connection

Having a spiritual community is important because we all need to be connected to others who support our belief systems. But even if you belong to a religious community, you should still strengthen your personal spiritual body. Just as you can learn things even when you are out of school, you can develop a very real spiritual life even if you are not connected to a religious organization.

There are several ways to develop your spiritual muscles.
(Check out Chapter 5, "The 42 Principles of Ma'at") As well as:

Praying

Have a conversation with the Creator. Strengthen your relationship by spending time giving thanks. Standing or kneeling before the Creator with your hands prayerfully joined is more than just something nice to do. It naturally prompts us to go within with humility.

No prayer is ever unheard or unanswered (sometimes the answer is "Yes," "No," or "Not now")

Libations

Libations are simply another form of prayer. Many different cultures around the world (including Africa) pour libations during ceremonies, celebrations, as well as family and community gatherings. It is a way of giving honor to our ancestors, our Motherland and to the Creator. In public settings, libations are usually performed by the eldest and most respected member of the family or community. A plant is typically used when indoors, to symbolize the earth and its life-sustaining qualities. Liquids like water or oil are used to symbolize the continual flow of life as well as to represent our spiritual connection.

When you pour libations, it should be done with the same respect as any other prayer. It is tradition to pour the water after each statement. Some statements that can be used are:

"For the Almighty Creator who makes all life possible"
("we pour libations")

"For our ancient ancestors who lived and died on the continent of Africa"
("we pour libations")

"For the countless freedom fighters that struggled and died on our behalf"
(Harriet Tubman, Dr. Martin Luther King, Jr., etc.)
("we pour libations")

"For our family ancestors who have made their transitions" (our parents, grandparents, and other family members)
("we pour libations")

"For our elders who guide us with their wisdom"
("we pour libations")

"For the youth and those yet to be born"
("we pour libations")

"For the principles that guide us on a daily basis"
("we pour libations")

No matter what form prayer takes, communicating with the Creator and remembering our ancestors makes us aware of being part of the human race from the past, through the present and into the future. It helps to wake up and grow our spiritual bodies. **Always remembering to remember...**

"What you can become, you already are."
- Ellen Glasgow

Phase Four: The Butterfly
Empowering Myself

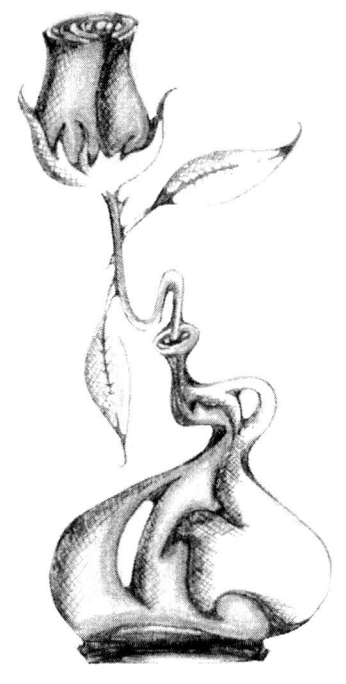

— Chapter 16 —

"Connecting With My Life Purpose"

Identifying My Gifts

There is for each person, the perfect self-expression. There are places for you to fill that no one else can fill, some things for you to do that no one else can do - they are called "Your Gifts." Everybody has at least one.

If we all have a purpose, why do we forget it? Well, not only do we come to the planet to bring our gifts, but we are also here to learn lessons as well.

Your physical life began when you were in your mother's womb. The key to life is to remember what you knew then (before birth) that you have forgotten.

Coming to the planet can be a pretty scary thing. As soon as you arrive, a doctor hangs you upside down by your heels and slaps you on the behind until you cry. You are unable to speak the language or do anything but eat and sleep. Everybody is bigger than you. When you finally learn how to walk and talk, everyone bosses you around and tells you all the things you can't do. For a few short years, you are able to be creative and express yourself. Just when life is getting good, you have to go to school. There you learn how to get along with others and follow even more rules. You spend a lot of time trying to fit in and make friends. It is enough to make us forget our original mission.

That which you are looking for is also looking for you.

Many times you can find your gifts in the things that you enjoy doing. The challenging thing is to remember and to not be afraid to live your dream. Because many adults have forgotten their gifts, they spend most of their lives working at jobs that they dislike. They think that they are either too old, or that it's too late to make a change. So they stay in jobs that make them miserable, wasting time doing things that they hate. They are full of fears, and they pass those fears on to other people.

You can design a life or have one designed for you by someone else.

Know that you are fully equipped for the Divine Plan for your life, if you maintain the courage to do it.

> **"Don't worry about what the world needs.
> Ask what makes you come alive and do that.
> Because what the world needs are people
> who have come alive."**
> -Howard Thurman

Some will ask, "If I am destined for greatness, how come I don't achieve greatness? If I have a purpose, how can I die without fulfilling it?" Well, it's like the story of: The Potter and the Clay.

The Potter and the Clay

Once upon a time a master potter was making an exquisite vase out of clay. While she is making this beautiful vase, the clay is looking around at all of the beautifully crafted pieces in the shop and begins to think, "Wow! Look at how beautiful. Look at the different colors and shapes. I wonder if I will look like that?" And as the potter begins to knead and pound and shape this piece of clay - the clay begins to complain. "Ouch!, that hurts! Why do you have to throw me around! Why do you have to flatten me out like a pancake? I thought you said you wanted to make me a vase?" And the clay begins to doubt its purpose and the potter. It gets stuck in the memory of the pain of being flattened and kneaded and tossed around. And it begins to protest. Still looking around at all of the other finely crafted pieces - questioning, complaining and doubting the entire time.

Comparing himself to the finished pieces, he begins to see himself as inferior, and becomes sad and depressed. Not tuning in to the fact that the potter is now building a vase. This piece is so precious to her that she has decided to hand-build it rather than put it on the wheel. The clay is unaware of the process. So he begins asking other unfinished lumps of clay what does he look like. And the other lumps of clay (who are in different stages of development themselves) look at the clay and say, "Man, that is messed up." "She is really doing a job on you!" "What did you do to her?" "You must have really made her mad." "We have never seen anything like it." (Remember, they have very little experience themselves.)

So the clay becomes even more depressed as it is being pulled and shaped by the master potter. It just goes through the entire process feeling more and more defeated and depressed. As pieces are cut off, he moves between sadness, anger and even betrayal.

When he is formed and shaped, he is now ready for the next phase of the process - firing in the kiln (which is an extremely hot oven) to transform it from a piece of clay into a ceramic vase. Because the clay is filled with anger, resentment and doubt, when it is exposed to the extreme heat, (which is designed to transform it into a beautiful vase), it begins to crack. Because it is still resisting the process. Still not trusting the Potter.

When it is taken out of the kiln, sometimes pieces can be repaired, and sometimes they can't. And when they can't, you have to recycle the clay and begin again.

What happened to the clay had nothing to do with its original potential and purpose. It just didn't trust the process.

Creating Time to Celebrate Your Life

Time. There never seems to be enough of it to do all of the things that need to get done. Look around and you will see many people stressed out, overextended, overworked, overbooked, over-committed and overwhelmed. It's enough to make you tired just thinking about it!

We live in a society that encourages us to go, go, go. We have cell phones, cordless phones, pagers, the Internet, fast food, caffeine and ATMs - all designed to keep us moving. Moving straight to the goal of exhaustion.

In African culture, our ancestors understood the natural cycles of life. They followed the examples of the animals and nature. Life is designed to be experienced in cycles and seasons. Because our bodies are closely tied to the earth, we would do well to pay attention to nature and grow in understanding about our body's natural cycles and rhythms. Many times we are filled with stress because we are going against the natural flow. As females, our monthly menstrual cycle is connected to the cycles of the moon (see Chapter 7). But even on a larger scale, our bodies are connected to the rhythms of the earth. Just as understanding your connection to the moon is important, understanding your connection with the earth is just as vital. Not understanding the rhythms of the earth is like trying to walk up an escalator that is going down.

Winter - Winter Solstice (December 20-23)

Living on this side of the planet (in the Northern Hemisphere), the Winter Solstice marks the longest night of the year. The sun is at its lowest point in the sky. Just as the earth is quiet, like a caterpillar in a cocoon, in the darkness of the night, the earth is resting as it prepares to bring forth new life in the spring. The earth covers itself with a blanket of snow, as the trees shake off their leaves. Winter is a natural time to slow down, rest, dream, reflect and plan for the future.

We become full of stress when we try to do the opposite of that in the winter. For many people, winter is one of the busiest times of the year. Instead of cocooning, we are encouraged to work harder, shop til we drop, and get into the hustle and bustle of the holiday season. What could be joyous celebrations of thanksgiving, typically turn out to be stress-filled days of spending and overeating. Most people start the Roman New Year (January 1st) completely stressed out and overextended with debts.

Use the winter to slow down instead of to speed up. Use the time to read, pray, plan and nurture yourself:
  • take warm baths • meditate • reflect on the past year (what lessons did you learn? what will you do differently in the new year?) • massage your scalp • treat your hair to a hot oil treatment • write a story, a play or a song • read inspiring books about other people • dare to dream

Winter is an excellent time to cocoon

Spring - Spring Equinox (March 20-23)

After the long nights of winter comes spring. During the Spring Equinox, day and nighttime are equal in length. The earth begins to wake up and warm up, bringing forth new life. Butterflies come out of their cocoons. Leaves and buds appear on the trees. Birds begin singing again as the days get longer. Everything is becoming alive. Love is in the air. Many people get "Spring Fever," making it hard to sit still. It's a celebration of new life.

As nature is experiencing a rebirth, spring is a wonderful time to experience a sense of new life and renewal. Use the natural energy of spring to cleanse and shed your winter covering.
• "spring clean" - go through all of your clothes and material possessions and give away those things that are no longer useful to you • throw away papers and unnecessary clutter • cleanse your internal system by fasting for a day • drink lots of water • celebrate and give thanks for this new beginning • get a new hair style • develop a new attitude • create a treasure map

Plant your creative seeds in the Spring

Summer - Summer Solstice (June 20-23)
Summertime! The Summer Solstice marks the time of the year when the sun is at its peak and the earth is full of life. The earth gives us nature's talent show as we witness it bringing forth its very best. The earth rolls out a green carpet for us to lay, sit and play on. Plants and the earth are bearing delicious fruits and vegetables, the water is warm and inviting, the sky is blue and full of birds and butterflies. Music is in the air. Enjoy the summer!
• do well in school so that you don't have to go to summer school • play • live your life with passion and purpose • enter a talent or art show • go to cultural festivals • learn to drum or to do african dance • bring out your journal from winter and spring, then look back and make sure you are moving in the direction of your goals

Create and celebrate abundance in the Summer

Fall - Fall Equinox (September 20-23)
Fall is the time of the year when the earth, after manifesting its very best in the summer, gives us an opportunity to gather and harvest. We get to witness the abundance of the earth and give thanks. Fall is the time that

we remember lessons we have learned. What do we want to grow next year in our lives? As the leaves on the trees change to beautiful shades of red, yellow and orange, ask yourself "What do I need to change?" Just as the caterpillar eats to prepare for the season in its cocoon, fall is a good time to return to school and expand our minds and hearts. Ants, squirrels and other animals gather the foods that will carry them through the winter. Are you emotionally, physically and spiritually in good shape? Are you prepared for the challenges ahead?

• Learn something new • eat less processed "fast foods" and more natural foods • be thankful • prepare for the winter (if you celebrate Christmas and Kwanzaa, begin planning for the gifts that you KNOW you will give - don't wait until winter • stay focused on your goals, so that when winter comes you will be ready

Prepare for Winter in the Fall

Every day the Creator gives us the sun, moon and the earth to show us how to live in cycles. These cycles affect us whether we pay attention or not. For everything there is a season. Winter is going to come whether we like it or not. The key to finding time to celebrate your life is creating balance. Use the energy of the season to fuel your life.

Write the songs of your life in the winter, rehearse them in the spring, perform them in the summer and celebrate the abundance in the fall.

Working With CP Time

How do you view time? Where did the term "CP" time come from? First, let me explain what I understand "CP" time to mean. "CP" is short for "Colored People's."

Our African ancestors (like many people around the world who are connected to mother earth) weren't tied to a clock. They looked at the sun, the moon, the stars and the seasons to determine time. They lived in the present, not in the future. It's hard to be "late" when life is happening right now, in the present. Our natural body rhythm is very closely tied to the rhythm of nature and the earth.

Unfortunately you will have to find a balance between what some call "CP" time and society's time. In this society, there is not much room for life to just "happen." Everything is scheduled. If you show up for work "when you get there," you probably won't have a job to "go to" for very long. Being "late" is considered disrespectful in this society. In order to succeed, you have to understand the rules. Time is something that we have all collectively agreed to live by. If you find that you are functioning and flowing on "CP" time create a balance by planning to be wherever you are going, a half hour early. That way, you can be "in the moment" and "on time."

**The wonderful gift that we can gain from "CP" time is:
wherever you are - be there**

Procrastination and the Gift of the Present

Many people deal with the frustrating habit of procrastination. Some people will use the excuse, "That's just the way I am. I've always been like that." That may be true, but I have never met a hungry baby that waits two hours before letting you know that they are ready to eat. Procrastination is a habit that can be changed if you choose to deal with the real causes.

We sometimes procrastinate the things we don't like doing but know that we have to. Procrastination is sometimes a mask we wear to hide our fears. Sometimes it hides our fear of making mistakes, our fear of change, our fear of being rejected or our fear of the unknown. Sometimes we can be as afraid of success as much or more than we are of failure.

When YOU procrastinate, what are you really afraid of?

Mostly what keeps us from doing the things we need to do (when we need to do them) are the excuses and the negative things we say to ourselves. Fear can paralyze you. And if you combine fear with poor time management and planning, it is amazing that we can get anything done.

You will often hear people say "I work better under pressure." They wait until the last minute to work on school or work assignments and projects, putting off everything until the very last minute. Then, when they can no longer delay what needs to be done, they spring into action. The truth is, people don't work better under pressure, THEY JUST WORK!

Sometimes I put off taking action because I want to do a "perfect" job. When I don't know what the perfect action is, I wait. I don't want to look bad, so I just keep putting it off. Sometimes I wait and wait until I absolutely have to do it. I'm able to get the job done, but at the expense of being stressed out and having to stay up all night, rushing to put it together or to complete it. It winds up not being my best work, because I haven't given myself enough time to make mistakes.

I've learned that the perfect solutions don't always show up first, often we have to risk making mistakes before we can get to them.

There are some things that no matter how long you put them off, you will still need to do them. Don't let fear rob you of time. There is an old African story of how senior lions catch a gazelle...

When lions grow old and can't hunt and run as fast as they used to, they have to teach the young cubs to hunt or the entire family will starve. The way they teach them to hunt deer and other animals that are bigger and faster than the young cubs is the same way that "fear" works.

The elder lions know that their young lions are no match for the lightning fast speed of young gazelles. The young cubs legs are not strong enough nor do they have the confidence to hunt bigger animals. And the older lion, because he can no longer run as fast, would never be able to catch the gazelles either.

The wise old lions know the **power of fear.**

All the animals have to come down to the water to drink. So they have their young lions hide in the tall grass on one side of the water, and they hide in the grass on the other side. When the gazelles come down to the water to drink and to cool themselves, the senior lions, who are too old to hunt, will lie in the grass and begin to roar. The mature lion's roar is ferocious and very scary.

The gazelles hear the ferocious sound of the senior lions' roar and they immediately run in the opposite direction! But guess what? The young lions are waiting for them! They run right into the jaws of the young lions. The old lions just lay in the grass and continue to roar. If the gazelles were to run in the direction of the old lions, they would definitely be able to get away. The old lions would be no match for the quick moving gazelles. All the old lions have is their roar.

Usually, the things we are afraid of are not as fierce as we believe them to be. The next time you are afraid, and fear stops you in your tracks, remember the old lions and **Go into the Roar!**

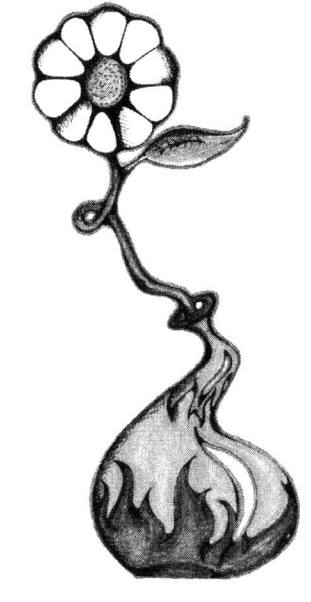

— Chapter 17 —

"*The Flow of Money*"

Making Peace With the Benjamins

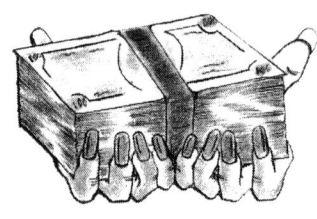

Money. It's important because, even though we are spiritual beings walking around in our mobile homes (our physical bodies), we have to move our bodies around the earth to collect life experiences. While we are doing that, we have to eat, sleep, wear clothes, and go to school. We need electricity, gas, heat, food and water. All of these things require money. It is a relationship we will have our entire lives.

Since money is one of our lifelong relationships, we might as well make the most of it. Try to get along with it and even become friends. Treat it with love and respect - just as you would any cherished friend. Don't fear it, ignore it (by pretending it doesn't exist), waste it, or hold on to it so tight that you hurt yourself and others. Learn to understand it, work with it, and of course, have fun with it.

Throughout history, money has gotten a bad rap. Many will kill, steal, lie, and cheat to get it. Because it has been associated with evil actions and misuses of power, many people have a lot of fear when dealing with it. People who have a lot of money are viewed by some as not being spiritual and good, and those who don't have a lot, are sometimes viewed as lazy and unworthy.

The truth is, money of itself is not good or bad. It is just a piece of paper or metal that we have all agreed to use as a symbol of appreciation. It only becomes negative when it is attached to negative emotions, like greed and deception that then create negative behaviors. Because we all have agreed to use little green pieces of paper as a means of exchange, we give it our energy. And truly, that is what money is - energy. Whatever you give energy to in your life will grow.

No matter what type of situation you were born into, you can always raise your level of income, because money is energy. Say it, "Money is energy." Say it again. Keep repeating it until you believe it. Once you

understand that you are full of energy and can generate energy, the sky is the limit! The ONLY thing that will stop you are your fears and what you believe about money. If you believe it to be anything other than energy, it will be difficult. You may find yourself being jealous and envious of others. You may even find yourself doing some crazy and unhealthy things to get it from others. The truth is:

The universe is rich and there is plenty for all.

The main key is, you can only receive what you can see yourself receiving. Wealth is not just reserved for a few special people. Within you lies all the talent, ideas and creativity you will ever need, to generate unlimited abundance for yourself.

Many times we will ask the Creator to send us money so that we can get out of debt or buy something that we really want. When millions of dollars don't immediately fall from the sky (or the lottery machine), we may think that our prayers haven't been heard and/or that we are being punished. The truth is, the Creator gives us something even more valuable - inspiration. It is up to us to turn the creative energy of our ideas into the energy of money. It is as if the Creator rains down little matchbooks of ideas everywhere. Your spirit ignites them when you fearlessly move into action.

If you chase after money, it can be a crazy ride - like trying to drive your car with a blindfold on. You may get where you are going but you are sure to do some serious damage along the way. But if you pursue your dreams and let the passion and inspiration that comes from the Creator lead your way - money is sure to flow. You are never given a dream without the power to make it come true. You will, however, have to work for it. And sometimes (most times), it's the "work" part that we don't really want to do.

It is not always going to be easy to follow your dreams. It will require lots of hard work, - not just physical, but emotional, mental and spiritual as well. Your creative inspirations (or dreams) will sometimes take you on a different path than most people are on. It may require you to spend many hours practicing or studying. You may have to change jobs, change friends, or move to a different city. In order to pursue your

dreams, you will have to make many sacrifices and never lose sight of your goal. It's not easy (that's why most people don't do it).

What will stop you dead in your tracks, are your FEARS and the FEARS of others. Fear will show up when you don't believe the inspirations from the Creator, or when you listen to other people and let them talk you out of what you feel divinely inspired to do.

For example, your life dream may be to sing. You love music. What if your voice is not all that hot - then what? Well, if you really feel that singing is your calling in life, before you spend money making a CD, you may want to take voice lessons. But, maybe you can do something else in the music industry. Maybe, instead of singing (or while you are taking lessons), you can earn money by working at a recording studio or radio station. Or maybe you can think of other creative ways to pursue your passion for music and earn a living at the same time. You may want to write songs, or produce them. Be flexible and creative. Don't be afraid to give yourself energy by taking different courses, paying attention to the many different ways you can make "music" and possibly earn money along the way.

If you maintain your creativity, and remember that your inspiration comes from the Creator, all things are possible. Listen to your "Intuition." You may have the solution to a problem. Or you may have an idea or the vision of how something can be done easier or better. Don't be afraid to follow your heart. Give your ideas and inspirations your "energy" and the "money energy" will follow (slowly, but surely). You may have an idea or an inspiration that could change the world, but you will have to believe in yourself (and convince others), in order to make it happen.

There is a supply for every demand.

Income vs. *Wealth*

Would you rather be "rich" or "wealthy"? What is the difference? Many times, people desire to "get rich quick" and look for different ways to make a whole lot of money in a short amount of time.

Income, is the cash flow that you generate from a job or a service that you offer - daily, weekly or monthly. Each time you get your paycheck - that's "income." You can make a lot of money, and buy many things. Most people "work to buy," spending more money then their income - creating large amounts of debt - living paycheck to paycheck. Cars, clothes, and things - you can spend your income buying anything and everything you want. Having money to spend can make you feel pretty important.

The bad news about "income" is that it can be stopped or cut off. You can lose your job. One day you can have a job that pays you so much money that you feel rich - and the next day you may be standing in the unemployment line. Can you still be "rich" without an "income"? Is your value tied to how much money you make? What if you lose your job - then what? How valuable are you?

"Wealth" is different than "income." Wealth equals the assets you have. No matter what happens, wealth will never go away. Being wealthy means more than just having a large quantity of things. It's a state of mind. Wealth is REALLY understanding that you are worth more than just your cash flow.

How do you build your assets? Concentrate on increasing your spiritual virtues and character. Having integrity, wisdom, compassion, honesty and wholeness are some of what makes up your REAL net worth. Once you understand that, you will be able to focus your energy on becoming what you really need and want to become - living to fulfill your life's mission. Creating wealth could look like you investing in yourself. For example, while working on a job, instead of using your INCOME to just purchase clothing, furniture and entertainment, let's say, you purchase "tools" that will help you to pursue your life mission.

This could also be considered building wealth. For example, a photographer I know, worked in the corporate world. While working the

job, his INCOME was good. He invested in his vision of being a photographer by purchasing cameras and other equipment. He also took classes related to his vision of being a photographer. When he lost his job, he had the means and skills to generate income.

Many people think of wealth as owning property and financial investments. But, one of the best ways to generate wealth, is by Investing in the Corporation of YOU.

The real measure of our wealth is how much we would be worth if we lost all our money.

"I have never been poor – only broke.
Being poor is a state of mind.
Being broke is only a temporary situation."
Author Unknown

— Chapter 18 —
"Cultural Diversity 101"

Dealing With Prejudice and Discrimination

There are a lot of things that aren't right in this world, and frankly, it all doesn't seem fair. There are many people who will treat you unfairly just because of the color of your skin and the way you look. And it's probably going to, at times, make you really, really angry. It can fill you with rage and hatred toward others. The key is - to channel that negative energy into fueling your mission. Because,
the best revenge is success.

Discrimination is something you will have to deal with. Period. I wish that life was setup differently - but it isn't. Discrimination has many faces: racial, sexual, gender and class. There will always be someone, somewhere who has a desire to treat you unfairly - for whatever reason. The important thing for you to remember is, discrimination and prejudice says more about the negative qualities of the "prejudice" person than about the person being "pre-judged". As our great, grandmothers used to say,
"Don't let what others eat, make you sick."

"They say that the bumblebee should not be able to fly. Her body is too big and her wings are too small to control her flight.

Yet, nobody has told the bumblebee, so therefore, she continues to fly."

There are no true obstacles to your achieving your dreams, life's mission and goals - except your fears and lack of faith in yourself. Others can only create hurdles for you to overcome. And you can overcome them! (If you don't give up.)

Do you know how circuses keep their adult elephants shackled to a small stake in the ground? The elephants are shackled to a stake when they are babies, and not very strong. The baby elephant struggles to get free - but he can't. He is not strong enough yet to break free from the stake in the ground.

Elephants have a great memory, so, as they grow bigger and stronger, they remember that when they were younger, they could not break free from the stake. So, the big powerful elephant doesn't even try to break free! He remembers the past, and doesn't even try, even though he is much stronger now than the small stake. He has been conditioned to not even fight against the stake.

People of African descent have a very painful history in this country. Our ancestors were brought here in shackles. During slavery, they were overpowered. Today, although we are much stronger as a group, many still remember the struggles of our ancestors and, don't even try to break free of the "shackles." The shackles remain, only now, instead of being attached to our physical bodies, they are attached to our minds. These "mental shackles" prevent many of us from showing up in life with our full strength.

We have strengths and qualities we don't even know we have or use because the memory of our ancestors' pain and enslavement is still strong. There are still some very powerful forces in this country that benefit from us not realizing how strong we are as a people. Just like the adult elephant, who doesn't realize his strength, we can choose to stay shackled in our minds, or we can realize our amazing power and strength and break free. For each person, it starts as a "mental thing."

We must never forget the struggles and pain of our ancestors, but what we should also remember is their incredible strength and determination. How do we break free from the "mental shackles" that continue to bind us? First, each individual person has to look inside himself and see where he is still shackled. Do you believe there are people who are "better" than you just because of the color of their skin? Do you give up on your dreams - even before you try? Are you afraid to fail? Do you sometimes wish you were born a different race? Do you feel like you are not as beautiful as other races?

It is very important to not forget our ancestors and the struggles of the past. Racism is still a strong force, and as long as we, like the circus elephant, remain unaware of our strength, things will stay the same. Don't forget the past, but also remember your gifts. Like the elephant, YOU ARE MUCH STRONGER THAN YOU THINK!

Are You a Carrot, an Egg or a Coffee Bean?

A certain daughter complained to her father about her life and how things have been so hard for her. She did not know how she was going to make it and she wanted to give up. She was tired of fighting and struggling. It seemed that just as one problem was solved, another arose.

Her father, a chef, took her to the kitchen, filled three pots with water and placed the fire on high. Soon, the three pots came to a boil. In one he placed carrots, in the other he placed eggs, and in the last he placed ground coffee beans. He let them sit and boil, without saying a word.

The daughter sucked her teeth and impatiently wondered what he was trying to do. She had problems, and he was making this strange concoction. In half an hour he walked over to the oven and turned down the fire. He pulled the carrots out and placed them in the bowl. He pulled the eggs out and placed them in the bowl. Then he ladled the coffee out and placed it in a bowl.

Turning to her he asked. "Darling what do you see?"

Smartly, she replied. "Carrots, eggs, and coffee."

He brought her closer and asked her to feel the carrots. She did, and noted that they were soft. He then asked her to take an egg and break it. After pulling off the shell, she observed the hard-boiled egg. Finally, he asked her to sip the coffee. Her face frowned from the strength of the coffee.

Humbly, she asked. "What does it mean Father?"

He explained. "Each of them faced the same adversity, 212 degrees of boiling water. However each reacted differently. The carrot went in strong, and hard, but after going through boiling water, it softened and became weak."

"The egg was fragile. A thick outer shell protected a liquid center. But after sitting through the boiling water, its inside became hardened."

"The coffee beans are unique however. After they were in the boiling water, they became stronger and richer." "Which are you?" he asked his daughter.

When adversity knocks on your door, how do you respond? Are you a carrot, an egg, or a coffee bean?

Are you the carrot that seems hard, but with the smallest amount of pain, adversity, or heat, you wilt and become soft with no strength?

Are you the egg, which starts off with a flexible heart and a fluid spirit. But after a death, a breakup, or prejudice and discrimination, you became hardened and stiff. Your shell looks the same, but you are so bitter and tough with a stiff spirit and heart, internally.

Or are you like the coffee bean? The bean does not get its peak and robust flavor until it reaches 212 degrees Fahrenheit. When the water gets the hottest, it just tastes better. When things are at their worst, do you get better? When the hour is the darkest, and your trials are their greatest, does your worship elevate you to another level?

How do you handle adversity? Are you a Carrot, an Egg, or a Coffee Bean?
--- Author Unknown

How Comfortable Are You With the Skin You're In?

Unfortunately, many times you will experience discrimination and prejudice from other people of color. It doesn't matter whether your skin tone is light or if it is dark. The battle has been going on since we have been in this country. It started when our ancestors were enslaved. Lighter skinned slaves were treated better. After many years of experiencing not having privileges or having special privileges based JUST on the color of your skin, it is easy to see why some would believe that "lighter is better." But guess what? Physical slavery for black folks ended a long time ago, but are we still operating from the mindset of slavery?

If your skin is lighter in complexion, some will say, "She thinks she's something." If you are darker in complexion, some will say, "She is so ugly." It's a crazy thing (when you really think about it). What do you think? Are you caught up in the "Skin Tone" war? What are YOUR beliefs around skin tone? (Remember, you are a spiritual being, having a physical experience. Your body is just your container - or house. Your building may be painted a certain shade on the outside, but is it more valuable than what's on the inside?)

No single group owns the copyright for beauty, intelligence, gifts and talents.

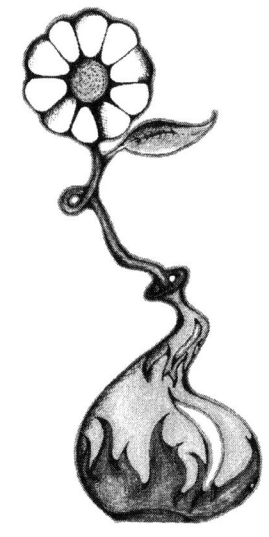

— *Chapter 19* —
"*Beyond the Butterfly*"

"What if I'm Pregnant or Have a Child – Is It Too Late For Me?"

Being a parent is one of the most challenging jobs on the planet. It is a big assignment. Not only are you responsible for learning your life lessons and bringing your gifts to the world, you have to make sure that your child learns its life lessons and bring its gifts into the world too.

If you are a teen parent, it can be even more difficult, because you have a parent who is also parenting you. It can be a pretty overwhelming experience. The important thing to remember, is that you are a spiritual being. The birth of your child will affect every aspect of your life.

Know that just as you are not a mistake, neither is your child. It is important that you understand, so you can communicate that knowledge to your child while he/she is in your womb and after they are born. It doesn't matter if you decide to keep your child or lovingly allow someone else to adopt - let your child know he or she is not a mistake. In other words, don't punish your child for the decisions you have made. All life comes from the Creator. Just as you came to fulfill a special purpose, so did your child.

You have a big job ahead of you - but you have the inner strength to do it - if you choose to. You can blame and punish yourself, the father of your child and others for the rest of your life, or you can look at where you are, and move forward.

It is never too late to be what you might have been.

"What Did You Say Your Baby's Name Is?"

Names. What the world calls you is very important. Names can hurt us, as well as inspire us to be our best. Names identify and set us apart from everyone else.

In African tradition, naming a newborn child was really significant. There were/are special ceremonies just for the purpose of naming a child and presenting him/her to the community. A newborn's name, spoke to either a characteristic of the child or his/her life's mission. So, naming a child was something that was done only after much thought, prayer and meditation. It marked the beginning of a child's physical life.

Today, because most African-Americans are not connected with African traditions, naming a child has become less significant. Many, in order to break away from typical Caucasian sounding names, create new names for their children. (Personally, I think it's a beautiful thing, because it is a
testimony to our continued creativity.)

The only down side (that I can see) is that many of the "new" names lack meaning (and that is very important). Sometimes, the names are made up
by advertisers or are just cute sounding with a unique spelling. Many are definitely original, however, everyone's name should mean something - because everyone's life has meaning and purpose.

What can you do? Well, if you have a child(ren) that have names that you have created, give them a special meaning. List all of the positive qualities you see in your child, and then choose the one characteristic that sticks out the most.

For example, what if you named your daughter "Tywanika." Take some time to quietly reflect on all the positive qualities you can see in your child or those that are not developed. If for instance, "Tywanika" cries a lot and needs lots of reassurance, if that is the one characteristic that stands out the most, maybe her name could mean "little brave one." As she grows, she will know that she can be brave (because that is the meaning of her name). Whenever she is afraid, she will remember the meaning of her name and grow in courage.

What if you or your child's name is associated with a product name? Names like Mercedes, Porche, Brandy, Lexus, or Tequilla are all beautiful sounding names, but are associated with cars and liquor. Since there is no rule stating that names can't have more than one meaning, you can still create a new meaning for a name. Who gives you the "authority" to do that? The Creator. Languages are just sounds that a collective group of people use in order to communicate. We all can agree that any group of letters form a word or a new meaning. Many words have multiple meanings, and words are being created all the time. The word "bad" for example, can mean something negative and it can mean something positive.

What if your name is unique and lacks a known meaning? First, you can ask your parents if your name has a known meaning. If the answer is "no" or your parents are not available, you can ask those who love you to list all of your positive qualities. Ask for their support in creating a meaning for your name. Ask the Creator to inspire you. Just as your name was inspired, ask for inspiration for its meaning. Listen, and expect an answer.

Once you have decided on a meaning for your or your child's name, create a special ceremony to celebrate. Ask a few close friends and relatives, to participate in supporting you. Ask the Creator for wisdom to guide you. Write the meaning down and remind yourself and your child often, of its unique and special meaning.

If you don't give yourself Energy, Health and Happiness - you won't be able to give it to your children.

— *Chapter 20* —

"Where Do I Go From Here?"

"Did I Get What I Needed – Or Am I Bound To Repeat It?"

Unfortunately, life is not designed to make you comfortable. Life is not a vacation. You came here to learn lessons and to bring gifts to the planet. As you go through life, you may wonder why you continue to go through the same types of challenges over and over again.

In school, there are some classes that you are required to pass before you can move on to the next grade. And just like in school, there are lessons that you as a spiritual being need to complete as a part of your "spiritual development curriculum."

The good news is, once you really learn the lesson, you don't have to continue repeating the experience. Life can get easier as you grow in self-understanding and wisdom.

Life doesn't have to be complicated – keep it simple.

Life is full of interesting twists and turns, and most times you will not be able to see all of the wonderful opportunities that are down the road by just standing where you are. Start walking in the direction of your dreams and the Creator will meet you along the path.

When a major shift, or change in direction occurs in your life, it means the supposed ending of something and also the beginning of something else. What might be ending is neither charged with positive energy nor negative energy. What is going to come is neutral. How you think about it will determine how you feel.

**There is nothing new under the sun,
It's all about how we reinterpret
what's already been done.**

I've Got a Plan

Plan your work - and then, work your plan.

Creating a vision for yourself is an important step to achieving your goals. If you wanted to build a house, you would need a blueprint or floor plan. What if you didn't have a blueprint when building your house? What if you told the builders and construction workers, "I don't care. Put the sink wherever you want. It doesn't matter. Whatever."

You can only imagine how your house would turn out. You've got to have a vision. Many of us don't have any problem envisioning our future, but many times we can briefly see all the positive and exciting things, and then we think of and dwell on, all the negative things or why we think our dreams can't and won't come true.

If you ask for success and then prepare for failure, you will get the situation you have prepared for.

Remember, your body is your mobile home that you get to use as you go along in life collecting experiences. The saying, "Life is a TRIP!" is very true. Life IS a trip. It is a journey. Just like any other road trip, it is a lot easier to get where you want to go, if you have a map.

Now, we all know that the world is round, so no matter where you are, if you keep walking, you will eventually get to your desired destination. Think of your city, for example. Let's say, you wanted to go to a friend's house. Instead of walking in the direction of your friend's home, you turn around and go in the opposite direction. It may take you hours, days, weeks months and even years to get there.

If you don't maintain your vision, you may eventually get to your goals, but it is sure to take a lot longer.

Plan with a purpose, and then Stick to the script.

— *Conclusion* —

The Bottom Line Is...

Unfortunately, life is not designed to make you comfortable - but to learn the lessons you agreed to come and learn. I (you) came to:
- learn lessons
- bring gifts to the planet

There are no mistakes. As you continue to go through your life, you will have many challenges to occur. It is important that you overcome them by setting goals, listening to your inner voice, asking for help when you need it (from people around you and your ancestors), and you will succeed - it's guaranteed.

Don't fill your luggage with a bunch of old negative tape.

Your Inner Child holds the keys to the door of your creativity, She won't give you the keys until you listen to her and love her. You have the power to change your past, your present and your future.

Always go for the "content" when dating.

Don't become a parent before you AND your future "Baby's Daddy" are ready: Emotionally, Physically, Mentally and Spiritually. It is one of the most important life decisions that you will ever make.

Be careful of the influences in the media.

Like a butterfly, you must be willing to journey into your dreams, your mind, your body and spirit - to find your true "Girl Power." You are a lot stronger than you think.

Your body is your vehicle for the entire time you are on the planet, so you have to take care of it and maintain it so it will support you your entire life.

Study yourself, so you can become an expert on the subject of YOU!

The two most important life-long relationships that you will always have are: with the Creator and with Yourself (cherish them both.)

Wisdom is knowing what to do with what you know.

What the Caterpillar calls the end of the world, is really the beginning of a Butterfly…

I take me,
to have and to hold,
from this day forward,
for better or for worse,
for richer, for poorer,
in sickness and
in health,
to love and to cherish,
til I depart in death,
so help me God.

I do.

Appendix

Perpetual Calendar

Use the tables below to find out which calendar you should use to identify the day of the week you were born. For example, if you were born in 1992, use calendar #K. Go to calendar #K and find your birth date and the day you were born. If your birth year is not listed below, visit: www.timeanddate.com/calendar/calendar

Use calendar #A if you were born in:
1961   1989
1967   1995
1978   2006

Use calendar #B if you were born in:
1962   1990
1973   2001
1979   2007

Use calendar #C if you were born in:
1963   1991
1974   2002
1985   2013

Use calendar #D if you were born in:
1969   1997
1975   2003
1986

Use calendar #E if you were born in:
1970   1998
1981   2009
1987

Use calendar #F if you were born in:
1965   1993
1971   1999
1982   2010

Use calendar #G if you were born in:
1966   1994
1977   2005
1983   2011

Use calendar #H if you were born in:
1984   2012

Use calendar #I if you were born in:
1968   1996

Use calendar #J if you were born in:
1980   2008

Use calendar #K if you were born in:
1964   1992

Use calendar #L if you were born in:
1976   2004

Use calendar #M if you were born in:
1960   1988

Use calendar #N if you were born in:
1972   2000

#A

January						
S	M	T	W	T	F	S
1	2	3	4	5	6	7
8	9	10	11	12	13	14
15	16	17	18	19	20	21
22	23	24	25	26	27	28
29	30	31				

February						
S	M	T	W	T	F	S
			1	2	3	4
5	6	7	8	9	10	11
12	13	14	15	16	17	18
19	20	21	22	23	24	25
26	27	28				

March						
S	M	T	W	T	F	S
			1	2	3	4
5	6	7	8	9	10	11
12	13	14	15	16	17	18
19	20	21	22	23	24	25
26	27	28	29	30	31	

April						
S	M	T	W	T	F	S
						1
2	3	4	5	6	7	8
9	10	11	12	13	14	15
16	17	18	19	20	21	22
23	24	25	26	27	28	29
30						

May						
S	M	T	W	T	F	S
	1	2	3	4	5	6
7	8	9	10	11	12	13
14	15	16	17	18	19	20
21	22	23	24	25	26	27
28	29	30	31			

June						
S	M	T	W	T	F	S
				1	2	3
4	5	6	7	8	9	10
11	12	13	14	15	16	17
18	19	20	21	22	23	24
25	26	27	28	29	30	

July						
S	M	T	W	T	F	S
						1
2	3	4	5	6	7	8
9	10	11	12	13	14	15
16	17	18	19	20	21	22
23	24	25	26	27	28	29
30	31					

August						
S	M	T	W	T	F	S
		1	2	3	4	5
6	7	8	9	10	11	12
13	14	15	16	17	18	19
20	21	22	23	24	25	26
27	28	29	30	31		

September						
S	M	T	W	T	F	S
					1	2
3	4	5	6	7	8	9
10	11	12	13	14	15	16
17	18	19	20	21	22	23
24	25	26	27	28	29	30

October						
S	M	T	W	T	F	S
1	2	3	4	5	6	7
8	9	10	11	12	13	14
15	16	17	18	19	20	21
22	23	24	25	26	27	28
29	30	31				

November						
S	M	T	W	T	F	S
			1	2	3	4
5	6	7	8	9	10	11
12	13	14	15	16	17	18
19	20	21	22	23	24	25
26	27	28	29	30		

December						
S	M	T	W	T	F	S
					1	2
3	4	5	6	7	8	9
10	11	12	13	14	15	16
17	18	19	20	21	22	23
24	25	26	27	28	29	30
31						

#B

January	February	March
S M T W T F S	S M T W T F S	S M T W T F S
1 2 3 4 5 6	1 2 3	1 2 3
7 8 9 10 11 12 13	4 5 6 7 8 9 10	4 5 6 7 8 9 10
14 15 16 17 18 19 20	11 12 13 14 15 16 17	11 12 13 14 15 16 17
21 22 23 24 25 26 27	18 19 20 21 22 23 24	18 19 20 21 22 23 24
28 29 30 31	25 26 27 28	25 26 27 28 29 30 31

April	May	June
S M T W T F S	S M T W T F S	S M T W T F S
1 2 3 4 5 6 7	1 2 3 4 5	1 2
8 9 10 11 12 13 14	6 7 8 9 10 11 12	3 4 5 6 7 8 9
15 16 17 18 19 20 21	13 14 15 16 17 18 19	10 11 12 13 14 15 16
22 23 24 25 26 27 28	20 21 22 23 24 25 26	17 18 19 20 21 22 23
29 30	27 28 29 30 31	24 25 26 27 28 29 30

July	August	September
S M T W T F S	S M T W T F S	S M T W T F S
1 2 3 4 5 6 7	1 2 3 4	1
8 9 10 11 12 13 14	5 6 7 8 9 10 11	2 3 4 5 6 7 8
15 16 17 18 19 20 21	12 13 14 15 16 17 18	9 10 11 12 13 14 15
22 23 24 25 26 27 28	19 20 21 22 23 24 25	16 17 18 19 20 21 22
29 30 31	26 27 28 29 30 31	23 24 25 26 27 28 29
		30

October	November	December
S M T W T F S	S M T W T F S	S M T W T F S
1 2 3 4 5 6	1 2 3	1
7 8 9 10 11 12 13	4 5 6 7 8 9 10	2 3 4 5 6 7 8
14 15 16 17 18 19 20	11 12 13 14 15 16 17	9 10 11 12 13 14 15
21 22 23 24 25 26 27	18 19 20 21 22 23 24	16 17 18 19 20 21 22
28 29 30 31	25 26 27 28 29 30	23 24 25 26 27 28 29
		30 31

#C

January
S	M	T	W	T	F	S
		1	2	3	4	5
6	7	8	9	10	11	12
13	14	15	16	17	18	19
20	21	22	23	24	25	26
27	28	29	30	31		

February
S	M	T	W	T	F	S
					1	2
3	4	5	6	7	8	9
10	11	12	13	14	15	16
17	18	19	20	21	22	23
24	25	26	27	28		

March
S	M	T	W	T	F	S
					1	2
3	4	5	6	7	8	9
10	11	12	13	14	15	16
17	18	19	20	21	22	23
24	25	26	27	28	29	30
31						

April
S	M	T	W	T	F	S
	1	2	3	4	5	6
7	8	9	10	11	12	13
14	15	16	17	18	19	20
21	22	23	24	25	26	27
28	29	30				

May
S	M	T	W	T	F	S
			1	2	3	4
5	6	7	8	9	10	11
12	13	14	15	16	17	18
19	20	21	22	23	24	25
26	27	28	29	30	31	

June
S	M	T	W	T	F	S
						1
2	3	4	5	6	7	8
9	10	11	12	13	14	15
16	17	18	19	20	21	22
23	24	25	26	27	28	29
30						

July
S	M	T	W	T	F	S
	1	2	3	4	5	6
7	8	9	10	11	12	13
14	15	16	17	18	19	20
21	22	23	24	25	26	27
28	29	30	31			

August
S	M	T	W	T	F	S
				1	2	3
4	5	6	7	8	9	10
11	12	13	14	15	16	17
18	19	20	21	22	23	24
25	26	27	28	29	30	31

September
S	M	T	W	T	F	S
1	2	3	4	5	6	7
8	9	10	11	12	13	14
15	16	17	18	19	20	21
22	23	24	25	26	27	28
29	30					

October
S	M	T	W	T	F	S
		1	2	3	4	5
6	7	8	9	10	11	12
13	14	15	16	17	18	19
20	21	22	23	24	25	26
27	28	29	30	31		

November
S	M	T	W	T	F	S
					1	2
3	4	5	6	7	8	9
10	11	12	13	14	15	16
17	18	19	20	21	22	23
24	25	26	27	28	29	30

December
S	M	T	W	T	F	S
1	2	3	4	5	6	7
8	9	10	11	12	13	14
15	16	17	18	19	20	21
22	23	24	25	26	27	28
29	30	31				

#D

January

S	M	T	W	T	F	S
			1	2	3	4
5	6	7	8	9	10	11
12	13	14	15	16	17	18
19	20	21	22	23	24	25
26	27	28	29	30	31	

February

S	M	T	W	T	F	S
						1
2	3	4	5	6	7	8
9	10	11	12	13	14	15
16	17	18	19	20	21	22
23	24	25	26	27	28	

March

S	M	T	W	T	F	S
						1
2	3	4	5	6	7	8
9	10	11	12	13	14	15
16	17	18	19	20	21	22
23	24	25	26	27	28	29
30	31					

April

S	M	T	W	T	F	S
		1	2	3	4	5
6	7	8	9	10	11	12
13	14	15	16	17	18	19
20	21	22	23	24	25	26
27	28	29	30			

May

S	M	T	W	T	F	S
				1	2	3
4	5	6	7	8	9	10
11	12	13	14	15	16	17
18	19	20	21	22	23	24
25	26	27	28	29	30	31

June

S	M	T	W	T	F	S
1	2	3	4	5	6	7
8	9	10	11	12	13	14
15	16	17	18	19	20	21
22	23	24	25	26	27	28
29	30					

July

S	M	T	W	T	F	S
		1	2	3	4	5
6	7	8	9	10	11	12
13	14	15	16	17	18	19
20	21	22	23	24	25	26
27	28	29	30	31		

August

S	M	T	W	T	F	S
					1	2
3	4	5	6	7	8	9
10	11	12	13	14	15	16
17	18	19	20	21	22	23
24	25	26	27	28	29	30
31						

September

S	M	T	W	T	F	S
	1	2	3	4	5	6
7	8	9	10	11	12	13
14	15	16	17	18	19	20
21	22	23	24	25	26	27
28	29	30				

October

S	M	T	W	T	F	S
			1	2	3	4
5	6	7	8	9	10	11
12	13	14	15	16	17	18
19	20	21	22	23	24	25
26	27	28	29	30	31	

November

S	M	T	W	T	F	S
						1
2	3	4	5	6	7	8
9	10	11	12	13	14	15
16	17	18	19	20	21	22
23	24	25	26	27	28	29
30						

December

S	M	T	W	T	F	S
	1	2	3	4	5	6
7	8	9	10	11	12	13
14	15	16	17	18	19	20
21	22	23	24	25	26	27
28	29	30	31			

#E

January
S M T W T F S
1 2 3
4 5 6 7 8 9 10
11 12 13 14 15 16 17
18 19 20 21 22 23 24
25 26 27 28 29 30 31

February
S M T W T F S
1 2 3 4 5 6 7
8 9 10 11 12 13 14
15 16 17 18 19 20 21
22 23 24 25 26 27 28

March
S M T W T F S
1 2 3 4 5 6 7
8 9 10 11 12 13 14
15 16 17 18 19 20 21
22 23 24 25 26 27 28
29 30 31

April
S M T W T F S
1 2 3 4
5 6 7 8 9 10 11
12 13 14 15 16 17 18
19 20 21 22 23 24 25
26 27 28 29 30

May
S M T W T F S
1 2
3 4 5 6 7 8 9
10 11 12 13 14 15 16
17 18 19 20 21 22 23
24 25 26 27 28 29 30
31

June
S M T W T F S
1 2 3 4 5 6
7 8 9 10 11 12 13
14 15 16 17 18 19 20
21 22 23 24 25 26 27
28 29 30

July
S M T W T F S
1 2 3 4
5 6 7 8 9 10 11
12 13 14 15 16 17 18
19 20 21 22 23 24 25
26 27 28 29 30 31

August
S M T W T F S
1
2 3 4 5 6 7 8
9 10 11 12 13 14 15
16 17 18 19 20 21 22
23 24 25 26 27 28 29
30 31

September
S M T W T F S
1 2 3 4 5
6 7 8 9 10 11 12
13 14 15 16 17 18 19
20 21 22 23 24 25 26
27 28 29 30

October
S M T W T F S
1 2 3
4 5 6 7 8 9 10
11 12 13 14 15 16 17
18 19 20 21 22 23 24
25 26 27 28 29 30 31

November
S M T W T F S
1 2 3 4 5 6 7
8 9 10 11 12 13 14
15 16 17 18 19 20 21
22 23 24 25 26 27 28
29 30

December
S M T W T F S
1 2 3 4 5
6 7 8 9 10 11 12
13 14 15 16 17 18 19
20 21 22 23 24 25 26
27 28 29 30 31

#F

January	February	March
S M T W T F S	S M T W T F S	S M T W T F S
1 2	1 2 3 4 5 6	1 2 3 4 5 6
3 4 5 6 7 8 9	7 8 9 10 11 12 13	7 8 9 10 11 12 13
10 11 12 13 14 15 16	14 15 16 17 18 19 20	14 15 16 17 18 19 20
17 18 19 20 21 22 23	21 22 23 24 25 26 27	21 22 23 24 25 26 27
24 25 26 27 28 29 30	28	28 29 30 31
31		

April	May	June
S M T W T F S	S M T W T F S	S M T W T F S
1 2 3	1	1 2 3 4 5
4 5 6 7 8 9 10	2 3 4 5 6 7 8	6 7 8 9 10 11 12
11 12 13 14 15 16 17	9 10 11 12 13 14 15	13 14 15 16 17 18 19
18 19 20 21 22 23 24	16 17 18 19 20 21 22	20 21 22 23 24 25 26
25 26 27 28 29 30	23 24 25 26 27 28 29	27 28 29 30
	30 31	

July	August	September
S M T W T F S	S M T W T F S	S M T W T F S
1 2 3	1 2 3 4 5 6 7	1 2 3 4
4 5 6 7 8 9 10	8 9 10 11 12 13 14	5 6 7 8 9 10 11
11 12 13 14 15 16 17	15 16 17 18 19 20 21	12 13 14 15 16 17 18
18 19 20 21 22 23 24	22 23 24 25 26 27 28	19 20 21 22 23 24 25
25 26 27 28 29 30 31	29 30 31	26 27 28 29 30

October	November	December
S M T W T F S	S M T W T F S	S M T W T F S
1 2	1 2 3 4 5 6	1 2 3 4
3 4 5 6 7 8 9	7 8 9 10 11 12 13	5 6 7 8 9 10 11
10 11 12 13 14 15 16	14 15 16 17 18 19 20	12 13 14 15 16 17 18
17 18 19 20 21 22 23	21 22 23 24 25 26 27	19 20 21 22 23 24 25
24 25 26 27 28 29 30	28 29 30	26 27 28 29 30 31
31		

#G

January						
S	M	T	W	T	F	S
						1
2	3	4	5	6	7	8
9	10	11	12	13	14	15
16	17	18	19	20	21	22
23	24	25	26	27	28	29
30	31					

February						
S	M	T	W	T	F	S
		1	2	3	4	5
6	7	8	9	10	11	12
13	14	15	16	17	18	19
20	21	22	23	24	25	26
27	28					

March						
S	M	T	W	T	F	S
		1	2	3	4	5
6	7	8	9	10	11	12
13	14	15	16	17	18	19
20	21	22	23	24	25	26
27	28	29	30	31		

April						
S	M	T	W	T	F	S
					1	2
3	4	5	6	7	8	9
10	11	12	13	14	15	16
17	18	19	20	21	22	23
24	25	26	27	28	29	30

May						
S	M	T	W	T	F	S
1	2	3	4	5	6	7
8	9	10	11	12	13	14
15	16	17	18	19	20	21
22	23	24	25	26	27	28
29	30	31				

June						
S	M	T	W	T	F	S
			1	2	3	4
5	6	7	8	9	10	11
12	13	14	15	16	17	18
19	20	21	22	23	24	25
26	27	28	29	30		

July						
S	M	T	W	T	F	S
					1	2
3	4	5	6	7	8	9
10	11	12	13	14	15	16
17	18	19	20	21	22	23
24	25	26	27	28	29	30
31						

August						
S	M	T	W	T	F	S
	1	2	3	4	5	6
7	8	9	10	11	12	13
14	15	16	17	18	19	20
21	22	23	24	25	26	27
28	29	30	31			

September						
S	M	T	W	T	F	S
				1	2	3
4	5	6	7	8	9	10
11	12	13	14	15	16	17
18	19	20	21	22	23	24
25	26	27	28	29	30	

October						
S	M	T	W	T	F	S
						1
2	3	4	5	6	7	8
9	10	11	12	13	14	15
16	17	18	19	20	21	22
23	24	25	26	27	28	29
30	31					

November						
S	M	T	W	T	F	S
		1	2	3	4	5
6	7	8	9	10	11	12
13	14	15	16	17	18	19
20	21	22	23	24	25	26
27	28	29	30			

December						
S	M	T	W	T	F	S
				1	2	3
4	5	6	7	8	9	10
11	12	13	14	15	16	17
18	19	20	21	22	23	24
25	26	27	28	29	30	31

#H

	January	
S M T W T F S		
1 2 3 4 5 6 7		
8 9 10 11 12 13 14		
15 16 17 18 19 20 21		
22 23 24 25 26 27 28		
29 30 31		

	February	
S M T W T F S		
1 2 3 4		
5 6 7 8 9 10 11		
12 13 14 15 16 17 18		
19 20 21 22 23 24 25		
26 27 28 29		

	March	
S M T W T F S		
1 2 3		
4 5 6 7 8 9 10		
11 12 13 14 15 16 17		
18 19 20 21 22 23 24		
25 26 27 28 29 30 31		

	April	
S M T W T F S		
1 2 3 4 5 6 7		
8 9 10 11 12 13 14		
15 16 17 18 19 20 21		
22 23 24 25 26 27 28		
29 30		

	May	
S M T W T F S		
1 2 3 4 5		
6 7 8 9 10 11 12		
13 14 15 16 17 18 19		
20 21 22 23 24 25 26		
27 28 29 30 31		

	June	
S M T W T F S		
1 2		
3 4 5 6 7 8 9		
10 11 12 13 14 15 16		
17 18 19 20 21 22 23		
24 25 26 27 28 29 30		

	July	
S M T W T F S		
1 2 3 4 5 6 7		
8 9 10 11 12 13 14		
15 16 17 18 19 20 21		
22 23 24 25 26 27 28		
29 30 31		

	August	
S M T W T F S		
1 2 3 4		
5 6 7 8 9 10 11		
12 13 14 15 16 17 18		
19 20 21 22 23 24 25		
26 27 28 29 30 31		

	September	
S M T W T F S		
1		
2 3 4 5 6 7 8		
9 10 11 12 13 14 15		
16 17 18 19 20 21 22		
23 24 25 26 27 28 29		
30		

	October	
S M T W T F S		
1 2 3 4 5 6		
7 8 9 10 11 12 13		
14 15 16 17 18 19 20		
21 22 23 24 25 26 27		
28 29 30 31		

	November	
S M T W T F S		
1 2 3		
4 5 6 7 8 9 10		
11 12 13 14 15 16 17		
18 19 20 21 22 23 24		
25 26 27 28 29 30		

	December	
S M T W T F S		
1		
2 3 4 5 6 7 8		
9 10 11 12 13 14 15		
16 17 18 19 20 21 22		
23 24 25 26 27 28 29		
30 31		

#1

January
S M T W T F S
1 2 3 4 5 6
7 8 9 10 11 12 13
14 15 16 17 18 19 20
21 22 23 24 25 26 27
28 29 30 31

February
S M T W T F S
1 2 3
4 5 6 7 8 9 10
11 12 13 14 15 16 17
18 19 20 21 22 23 24
25 26 27 28 29

March
S M T W T F S
1 2
3 4 5 6 7 8 9
10 11 12 13 14 15 16
17 18 19 20 21 22 23
24 25 26 27 28 29 30
31

April
S M T W T F S
1 2 3 4 5 6
7 8 9 10 11 12 13
14 15 16 17 18 19 20
21 22 23 24 25 26 27
28 29 30

May
S M T W T F S
1 2 3 4
5 6 7 8 9 10 11
12 13 14 15 16 17 18
19 20 21 22 23 24 25
26 27 28 29 30 31

June
S M T W T F S
1
2 3 4 5 6 7 8
9 10 11 12 13 14 15
16 17 18 19 20 21 22
23 24 25 26 27 28 29
30

July
S M T W T F S
1 2 3 4 5 6
7 8 9 10 11 12 13
14 15 16 17 18 19 20
21 22 23 24 25 26 27
28 29 30 31

August
S M T W T F S
1 2 3
4 5 6 7 8 9 10
11 12 13 14 15 16 17
18 19 20 21 22 23 24
25 26 27 28 29 30 31

September
S M T W T F S
1 2 3 4 5 6 7
8 9 10 11 12 13 14
15 16 17 18 19 20 21
22 23 24 25 26 27 28
29 30

October
S M T W T F S
1 2 3 4 5
6 7 8 9 10 11 12
13 14 15 16 17 18 19
20 21 22 23 24 25 26
27 28 29 30 31

November
S M T W T F S
1 2
3 4 5 6 7 8 9
10 11 12 13 14 15 16
17 18 19 20 21 22 23
24 25 26 27 28 29 30

December
S M T W T F S
1 2 3 4 5 6 7
8 9 10 11 12 13 14
15 16 17 18 19 20 21
22 23 24 25 26 27 28
29 30 31

#J

January	February	March
S M T W T F S	S M T W T F S	S M T W T F S
1 2 3 4 5	1 2	1
6 7 8 9 10 11 12	3 4 5 6 7 8 9	2 3 4 5 6 7 8
13 14 15 16 17 18 19	10 11 12 13 14 15 16	9 10 11 12 13 14 15
20 21 22 23 24 25 26	17 18 19 20 21 22 23	16 17 18 19 20 21 22
27 28 29 30 31	24 25 26 27 28 29	23 24 25 26 27 28 29
		30 31

April	May	June
S M T W T F S	S M T W T F S	S M T W T F S
1 2 3 4 5	1 2 3	1 2 3 4 5 6 7
6 7 8 9 10 11 12	4 5 6 7 8 9 10	8 9 10 11 12 13 14
13 14 15 16 17 18 19	11 12 13 14 15 16 17	15 16 17 18 19 20 21
20 21 22 23 24 25 26	18 19 20 21 22 23 24	22 23 24 25 26 27 28
27 28 29 30	25 26 27 28 29 30 31	29 30

July	August	September
S M T W T F S	S M T W T F S	S M T W T F S
1 2 3 4 5	1 2	1 2 3 4 5 6
6 7 8 9 10 11 12	3 4 5 6 7 8 9	7 8 9 10 11 12 13
13 14 15 16 17 18 19	10 11 12 13 14 15 16	14 15 16 17 18 19 20
20 21 22 23 24 25 26	17 18 19 20 21 22 23	21 22 23 24 25 26 27
27 28 29 30 31	24 25 26 27 28 29 30	28 29 30
	31	

October	November	December
S M T W T F S	S M T W T F S	S M T W T F S
1 2 3 4	1	1 2 3 4 5 6
5 6 7 8 9 10 11	2 3 4 5 6 7 8	7 8 9 10 11 12 13
12 13 14 15 16 17 18	9 10 11 12 13 14 15	14 15 16 17 18 19 20
19 20 21 22 23 24 25	16 17 18 19 20 21 22	21 22 23 24 25 26 27
26 27 28 29 30 31	23 24 25 26 27 28 29	28 29 30 31
	30	

#K

January						
S	M	T	W	T	F	S
			1	2	3	4
5	6	7	8	9	10	11
12	13	14	15	16	17	18
19	20	21	22	23	24	25
26	27	28	29	30	31	

February						
S	M	T	W	T	F	S
						1
2	3	4	5	6	7	8
9	10	11	12	13	14	15
16	17	18	19	20	21	22
23	24	25	26	27	28	29

March						
S	M	T	W	T	F	S
1	2	3	4	5	6	7
8	9	10	11	12	13	14
15	16	17	18	19	20	21
22	23	24	25	26	27	28
29	30	31				

April						
S	M	T	W	T	F	S
			1	2	3	4
5	6	7	8	9	10	11
12	13	14	15	16	17	18
19	20	21	22	23	24	25
26	27	28	29	30		

May						
S	M	T	W	T	F	S
					1	2
3	4	5	6	7	8	9
10	11	12	13	14	15	16
17	18	19	20	21	22	23
24	25	26	27	28	29	30
31						

June						
S	M	T	W	T	F	S
	1	2	3	4	5	6
7	8	9	10	11	12	13
14	15	16	17	18	19	20
21	22	23	24	25	26	27
28	29	30				

July						
S	M	T	W	T	F	S
			1	2	3	4
5	6	7	8	9	10	11
12	13	14	15	16	17	18
19	20	21	22	23	24	25
26	27	28	29	30	31	

August						
S	M	T	W	T	F	S
						1
2	3	4	5	6	7	8
9	10	11	12	13	14	15
16	17	18	19	20	21	22
23	24	25	26	27	28	29
30	31					

September						
S	M	T	W	T	F	S
		1	2	3	4	5
6	7	8	9	10	11	12
13	14	15	16	17	18	19
20	21	22	23	24	25	26
27	28	29	30			

October						
S	M	T	W	T	F	S
				1	2	3
4	5	6	7	8	9	10
11	12	13	14	15	16	17
18	19	20	21	22	23	24
25	26	27	28	29	30	31

November						
S	M	T	W	T	F	S
1	2	3	4	5	6	7
8	9	10	11	12	13	14
15	16	17	18	19	20	21
22	23	24	25	26	27	28
29	30					

December						
S	M	T	W	T	F	S
		1	2	3	4	5
6	7	8	9	10	11	12
13	14	15	16	17	18	19
20	21	22	23	24	25	26
27	28	29	30	31		

#L

January						
S	M	T	W	T	F	S
				1	2	3
4	5	6	7	8	9	10
11	12	13	14	15	16	17
18	19	20	21	22	23	24
25	26	27	28	29	30	31

February						
S	M	T	W	T	F	S
1	2	3	4	5	6	7
8	9	10	11	12	13	14
15	16	17	18	19	20	21
22	23	24	25	26	27	28
29						

March						
S	M	T	W	T	F	S
	1	2	3	4	5	6
7	8	9	10	11	12	13
14	15	16	17	18	19	20
21	22	23	24	25	26	27
28	29	30	31			

April						
S	M	T	W	T	F	S
				1	2	3
4	5	6	7	8	9	10
11	12	13	14	15	16	17
18	19	20	21	22	23	24
25	26	27	28	29	30	

May						
S	M	T	W	T	F	S
						1
2	3	4	5	6	7	8
9	10	11	12	13	14	15
16	17	18	19	20	21	22
23	24	25	26	27	28	29
30	31					

June						
S	M	T	W	T	F	S
		1	2	3	4	5
6	7	8	9	10	11	12
13	14	15	16	17	18	19
20	21	22	23	24	25	26
27	28	29	30			

July						
S	M	T	W	T	F	S
				1	2	3
4	5	6	7	8	9	10
11	12	13	14	15	16	17
18	19	20	21	22	23	24
25	26	27	28	29	30	31

August						
S	M	T	W	T	F	S
1	2	3	4	5	6	7
8	9	10	11	12	13	14
15	16	17	18	19	20	21
22	23	24	25	26	27	28
29	30	31				

September						
S	M	T	W	T	F	S
			1	2	3	4
5	6	7	8	9	10	11
12	13	14	15	16	17	18
19	20	21	22	23	24	25
26	27	28	29	30		

October						
S	M	T	W	T	F	S
					1	2
3	4	5	6	7	8	9
10	11	12	13	14	15	16
17	18	19	20	21	22	23
24	25	26	27	28	29	30
31						

November						
S	M	T	W	T	F	S
	1	2	3	4	5	6
7	8	9	10	11	12	13
14	15	16	17	18	19	20
21	22	23	24	25	26	27
28	29	30				

December						
S	M	T	W	T	F	S
		1	2	3	4	
5	6	7	8	9	10	11
12	13	14	15	16	17	18
19	20	21	22	23	24	25
26	27	28	29	30	31	

#M

January						
S	M	T	W	T	F	S
					1	2
3	4	5	6	7	8	9
10	11	12	13	14	15	16
17	18	19	20	21	22	23
24	25	26	27	28	29	30
31						

February						
S	M	T	W	T	F	S
	1	2	3	4	5	6
7	8	9	10	11	12	13
14	15	16	17	18	19	20
21	22	23	24	25	26	27
28	29					

March						
S	M	T	W	T	F	S
		1	2	3	4	5
6	7	8	9	10	11	12
13	14	15	16	17	18	19
20	21	22	23	24	25	26
27	28	29	30	31		

April						
S	M	T	W	T	F	S
					1	2
3	4	5	6	7	8	9
10	11	12	13	14	15	16
17	18	19	20	21	22	23
24	25	26	27	28	29	30

May						
S	M	T	W	T	F	S
1	2	3	4	5	6	7
8	9	10	11	12	13	14
15	16	17	18	19	20	21
22	23	24	25	26	27	28
29	30	31				

June						
S	M	T	W	T	F	S
			1	2	3	4
5	6	7	8	9	10	11
12	13	14	15	16	17	18
19	20	21	22	23	24	25
26	27	28	29	30		

July						
S	M	T	W	T	F	S
					1	2
3	4	5	6	7	8	9
10	11	12	13	14	15	16
17	18	19	20	21	22	23
24	25	26	27	28	29	30
31						

August						
S	M	T	W	T	F	S
	1	2	3	4	5	6
7	8	9	10	11	12	13
14	15	16	17	18	19	20
21	22	23	24	25	26	27
28	29	30	31			

September						
S	M	T	W	T	F	S
				1	2	3
4	5	6	7	8	9	10
11	12	13	14	15	16	17
18	19	20	21	22	23	24
25	26	27	28	29	30	

October						
S	M	T	W	T	F	S
						1
2	3	4	5	6	7	8
9	10	11	12	13	14	15
16	17	18	19	20	21	22
23	24	25	26	27	28	29
30	31					

November						
S	M	T	W	T	F	S
		1	2	3	4	5
6	7	8	9	10	11	12
13	14	15	16	17	18	19
20	21	22	23	24	25	26
27	28	29	30			

December						
S	M	T	W	T	F	S
				1	2	3
4	5	6	7	8	9	10
11	12	13	14	15	16	17
18	19	20	21	22	23	24
25	26	27	28	29	30	31

#N

	January					
S	M	T	W	T	F	S
						1
2	3	4	5	6	7	8
9	10	11	12	13	14	15
16	17	18	19	20	21	22
23	24	25	26	27	28	29
30	31					

	February					
S	M	T	W	T	F	S
		1	2	3	4	5
6	7	8	9	10	11	12
13	14	15	16	17	18	19
20	21	22	23	24	25	26
27	28	29				

	March					
S	M	T	W	T	F	S
		1	2	3	4	5
6	7	8	9	10	11	12
13	14	15	16	17	18	19
20	21	22	23	24	25	26
27	28	29	30	31		

	April					
S	M	T	W	T	F	S
						1
2	3	4	5	6	7	8
9	10	11	12	13	14	15
16	17	18	19	20	21	22
23	24	25	26	27	28	29
30						

	May					
S	M	T	W	T	F	S
	1	2	3	4	5	6
7	8	9	10	11	12	13
14	15	16	17	18	19	20
21	22	23	24	25	26	27
28	29	30	31			

	June					
S	M	T	W	T	F	S
				1	2	3
4	5	6	7	8	9	10
11	12	13	14	15	16	17
18	19	20	21	22	23	24
25	26	27	28	29	30	

	July					
S	M	T	W	T	F	S
						1
2	3	4	5	6	7	8
9	10	11	12	13	14	15
16	17	18	19	20	21	22
23	24	25	26	27	28	29
30	31					

	August					
S	M	T	W	T	F	S
		1	2	3	4	5
6	7	8	9	10	11	12
13	14	15	16	17	18	19
20	21	22	23	24	25	26
27	28	29	30	31		

	September					
S	M	T	W	T	F	S
					1	2
3	4	5	6	7	8	9
10	11	12	13	14	15	16
17	18	19	20	21	22	23
24	25	26	27	28	29	30

	October					
S	M	T	W	T	F	S
1	2	3	4	5	6	7
8	9	10	11	12	13	14
15	16	17	18	19	20	21
22	23	24	25	26	27	28
29	30	31				

	November					
S	M	T	W	T	F	S
			1	2	3	4
5	6	7	8	9	10	11
12	13	14	15	16	17	18
19	20	21	22	23	24	25
26	27	28	29	30		

	December					
S	M	T	W	T	F	S
					1	2
3	4	5	6	7	8	9
10	11	12	13	14	15	16
17	18	19	20	21	22	23
24	25	26	27	28	29	30
31						

About the Author

Since it's original printing in 2003, the book Project Butterfly has inspired the creation of a national non-profit organization - Camp Butterfly. In 2004, Ms. Jaha-Echols founded Camp Butterfly, an organization focusing on the culturally specific needs of women and girls of African descent and their unique developmental and emotional needs. Through its residential summer camp experiences and its year round programming, Camp Butterfly serves women and girls from across the country.

As a consultant and inspirational speaker, Niambi has facilitated sessions for public schools, private agencies, juvenile detention centers, and various colleges and universities across the country.

For more information on Project Butterfly visit:
www.projectbutterfly.com
www.perfectbookspublishing.com

For more information on Camp Butterfly, visit: www.campbutterfly.org

To contact Niambi Jaha-Echols regarding speaking engagements:
Email: niambi@projectbutterfly.com
www.niambijaha.com
(773) 457-0114

All written correspondence should be directed to:
Niambi Jaha-Echols
c/o Perfect Books Publishing
7439 S. Bennett Avenue
Chicago, IL 60649
www.perfectbookspublishing.com